For I Know The Plans

NAVIGATING THROUGH THE TUNNEL OF LOSS

AMY BIRCHFIELD

Foreword by
Tammy Melton, LAPC

authorHOUSE

AuthorHouse™
1663 Liberty Drive
Bloomington, IN 47403
www.authorhouse.com
Phone: 1 (800) 839-8640

© 2015 AMY BIRCHFIELD. All rights reserved.

No part of this book may be reproduced, stored in a retrieval system, or transmitted by any means without the written permission of the author.

Published by AuthorHouse   10/30/2015

ISBN: 978-1-5049-5045-9 (sc)
ISBN: 978-1-5049-5044-2 (hc)
ISBN: 978-1-5049-5046-6 (e)

Library of Congress Control Number: 2015915481

Print information available on the last page.

Any people depicted in stock imagery provided by Thinkstock are models, and such images are being used for illustrative purposes only.
Certain stock imagery © Thinkstock.

This book is printed on acid-free paper.

Because of the dynamic nature of the Internet, any web addresses or links contained in this book may have changed since publication and may no longer be valid. The views expressed in this work are solely those of the author and do not necessarily reflect the views of the publisher, and the publisher hereby disclaims any responsibility for them.

Contact Information
www.AuthorAmyBirchfield.com
To order books and receive
more information

AuthorAmyBirchfield@gmail.com
To submit questions, to give Amy
feedback on your experiences, and/
or to request Amy for speaking
at your upcoming event

THE HOLY BIBLE, NEW INTERNATIONAL VERSION®, NIV® Copyright © 1973, 1978, 1984, 2011 by Biblica, Inc.™ Used by permission. All rights reserved worldwide.

"Scripture quotations taken from the New American Standard Bible®, Copyright © 1960, 1962, 1963, 1968, 1971, 1972, 1973, 1975, 1977, 1995 by The Lockman Foundation Used by permission." (www.Lockman.org)

"Scripture quotations taken from the Amplified® Bible, Copyright © 1954, 1958, 1962, 1964, 1965, 1987 by The Lockman Foundation Used by permission." (www.Lockman.org)

Scripture quotations from THE MESSAGE. Copyright © by Eugene H. Peterson 1993, 1994, 1995, 1996, 2000, 2001, 2002. Used by permission of Tyndale House Publishers, Inc.

"Scripture taken from the New Century Version®. Copyright © 2005 by Thomas Nelson, Inc. Used by permission. All rights reserved."

Scripture quotations are taken from the *Holy Bible*, New Living Translation, copyright ©1996, 2004, 2007, 2013 by Tyndale House Foundation. Used by permission of Tyndale House Publishers, Inc., Carol Stream, Illinois 60188. All rights reserved.

Scripture is taken from GOD'S WORD®, © 1995 God's Word to the Nations. Used by permission of Baker Publishing Group.

Scripture taken from the New King James Version®. Copyright © 1982 by Thomas Nelson. Used by permission. All rights reserved.

*This book is dedicated to my Daddy God.
Lord, I give You all the glory and honor
for my life and for giving me the grace and
love to navigate through this journey.
&
My beloved Raymon
Raymon, Thank you for joining me on a
journey of love that has taught me many lessons
which have shaped my heart forever.
I love you always!*

Dearest Friend,

This book has been a labor of love. It was difficult to write and open up about the greatest heartbreak of my life. I somehow felt my private heart was now open to a public world. This was scary for me but I did it for you— in hopes that sharing my heart and life with you would give you the strength and hope to fulfill that which God has called you to do on your journey.

I know it is very difficult to travel through the tunnel of loss. If I could be there with you now in person, I would hold your hands, look into your beautiful eyes and say "I know the pain and you will make it through this. Please keep your hand in God's hand because He does know the plans for you. They are good and He loves you like no other."

Contents

Foreword xv
Acknowledgements xxiii
Prologue: My Princess Story xxvii

Chapter 1   An Army of One 1
Chapter 2   The Entrance Into My Tunnel 43
Chapter 3   Glorify And Honor 57
Chapter 4   Depending On God 79
Chapter 5   Identity Crisis 101
Chapter 6   People Within Our Tunnel 123
Chapter 7   Forgiveness Brings Freedom 139
Chapter 8   One Day At A Time 161
Chapter 9   Time-Out 175
Chapter 10 Maintaining Life 183
Chapter 11 Celebrating Memories 199
Chapter 12 The Golden Key 209
Chapter 13 Beckoning Light 221

About the Author 247

To my family: "Thank you for your love and support."

Travel with me to the songs of my life:

(Listed in the order of mention)

Music has been and is such an important part of my life. I believe that listening to these songs will give you a deeper insight through my life and story.

Prologue
"Jesu, Joy of Man's Desiring" – JS Bach
"Make Us One" – Carol Cymbala (choir director for the Brooklyn Tabernacle Choir)
"From This Moment On" – Shania Twain
"Trumpet Voluntary" – Jeremiah Clarke
"The Power of Love" – Celine Dion (co-written by Jennifer Rush)
"My Special Angel" – Bobby Helms (written by Jimmy Duncan)
"Because You Loved Me" – Celine Dion (written by Diane Warren)

Chapter I – An Army of One
"My Special Angel" – Bobby Helms (written my Jimmy Duncan)
"You Raise Me Up" – Josh Groban (written by Brendan Graham)
"God Bless the USA" – Lee Greenwood
"Star Spangled Banner" – John Stafford Smith (written by Francis Scott Key)
"Blessed Be Your Name" – Matt Redman
"Love Me" – Frances Drost
"Achy Breaky Heart" – Billy Ray Cyrus (written by Don Von Tress)
"You Light Up My Life" – Debby Boone (written by Joseph Brooks)

Chapter II—The Entrance Into My Tunnel
"The Dance"—*Garth Brooks (written by Tony Arata)*
"Praise You In This Storm"—*Casting Crowns*

Chapter III—Glorify and Honor
"God Bless the USA"—*Lee Greenwood*
"Star Spangled Banner"—*John Stafford Smith (written by Francis Scott Key)*
"Taps"—*Daniel Butterfield (While writing this book I discovered that the first sounding of Taps at a military funeral is commemorated in a stained glass window at The Chapel of the Centurion (The Old Post Chapel) at Fort Monroe, Virginia-the post where Raymon asked me to marry him.)*
"Victory In Jesus"—*Eugene M. Bartlett Sr.(The last hymn Mr. Bartlett wrote after he had suffered a stroke.)*
"Splish Splash"—*Bobby Darin*
"Old Time Rock and Roll"—*Bob Seger*
"The Power of Love"—*Celine Dion (co-written by Jennifer Rush)*
"My Special Angel"—*Bobby Helms (written by Jimmy Duncan)*
"You Light Up My Life"—*Debby Boone (written by Joseph Brooks)*
"Wind Beneath My Wings"—*Bette Midler (written by Larry Henley and Jeff Silbar)*
"Rockin' Robin"—*Bobby Day*
"Days of Elijah"—*Robin Mark*
"Shout To The Lord"—*Darlene Zschech*
"Taps"—*Daniel Butterfield*
"My Special Angel"—*Bobby Helms (written by Jimmy Duncan)*
"I Can Only Imagine"—*Mercy Me*
"Untitled Hymn"—*Chris Rice*
"Faith of Our Fathers"—*Frederick William Faber*

Chapter IV—Depending On God
"More"—Matthew West
"Victory"—Tye Tribbett (written by Ronan Hardiman)
"I Want It Back"—Tye Tribbett & GA
"I Can Only Imagine"—Mercy Me
"In Christ Alone"—Michael English (written by Stuart Townend)
"How Great Thou Art"—Stuart K. Hine
"Solid Rock"—Edward Mote

Chapter V—Identity Crisis
"Who Am I"—Casting Crowns

Chapter VI—People Within Our Tunnel
"Bless The Broken Road"—Rascal Flatts (written by Marcus Hummon, Bobby Boyd, and Jeff Hanna)
"My Wish"—Rascal Flatts (written by Jeffrey Stelle and Steve Robson)

Chapter VII—Forgiveness Brings Freedom
"Forgiven"—Matthew West

Chapter VIII—One Day At A Time
"The Proof of Your Love"—For King and Country

Chapter IX—Time-Out
"Be Still, My Soul"—Kathrina Von Schlegel

Chapter X—Maintaining Life
"I Surrender All"—J.W. Van DeVenter

Chapter XI—Celebrating Memories
"My Special Angel"—Bobby Helms (written by Jimmy Duncan)
"The Lion Sleeps Tonight"—The Tokens (written by Soloman Linda)
"Holly Jolly Christmas"—Burl Ives (written by Johnny Marks)
"I Will Rise"—Chris Tomlin

Chapter XII—The Golden Key
"Make Me a Channel of Your Peace"—attributed to St. Francis of Assisi

Chapter XIII—Beckoning Light
"Before The Morning"—Josh Wilson
"Home"—Michael Bublé
"The Rose"—Bette Midler (written by Amanda McBroom)
"Who Am I"—Casting Crowns
"Be Still and Know"—Steven Curtis Chapman
"Amazing Grace"—Harmonious Joy (The duo name for Scott and Amy Birchfield)
"While I'm Waiting"—John Waller
"Agnus Dei"—Michael W. Smith
"Love of My Life"—Michael W. Smith (written by Tom Douglas and Jim Brickman)
"I Won't Let Go"—Rascal Flatts (written by Steve Robson and Jason Sellers)
"Take My Hand, Precious Lord"—Rev. Thomas A. Dorsey

Foreword

No doubt about it, life can be hard! Jesus said that we would face trials: "These things I have spoken to you, that in Me you may have peace. In the world you will have tribulation; but be of good cheer, I have overcome the world" (John 16:33, NKJV). The problem comes when, in our human tendencies, we get stuck just focusing on the storms of life instead of the promise of God to bring us through. As you read this book, you will be reminded that God not only has a light for us at the end of the tunnel, but He also brings His rays of light into the tunnel of grief and brings peace and joy in the midst of pain.

This book starts out with the personal life story of Amy George (Birchfield) and her experiences as a military wife of a wounded soldier who struggled with severe PTSD which ultimately led to his death.

Amy tells her story in such a way that will draw you in and make you feel as if you have known the family for years. As I read the manuscript, I did not want to put it down, because I wanted to know how the narrative continued to unfold and how God orchestrated this beautiful story.

Amy masterfully crafted this manuscript not only to tell what happened in her own life, but especially to help you learn what to do when life is hard. She offers spiritual insight and practical advice to help you in your journey to freedom. It is as if she takes you by the hand and says, "I know you hurt! I have been there. Let me walk with you through this time and share with you what God taught me through my tunnel of grief. God will bring you through!"

As a professional counselor, I look forward to having *For I Know the Plans* as a resource for my clients. Not only will this book benefit people who are grieving the loss of loved ones, it will also help those who do not know what to say or do to help a friend who is in a time of mourning.

> Tammy Melton, LAPC
> www.legacyministries.info

Tammy Melton and Amy Birchfield

The Artist's Heart

I have felt God's leading through my journey in writing this book every step of the way. The cover of this book is a testament to that. I was at the headquarters of Legacy Ministries, the ministry that my friend Tammy and her husband Bill founded, for their regularly scheduled noon Friday prayer and worship when God spoke to my heart about Dee painting the artwork for the cover of my book.

I had asked that we pray for Dee because she had suddenly lost her husband just a week prior. As we were praying for Dee I was admiring her beautiful painting hanging on the wall that Dee was inspired to paint. It was based on one of her favorite verses quoted at the end of her message to you.

After we prayed for her, God spoke to my heart that she was to paint the artwork for the cover of this book and share from her heart her testimony. A couple of weeks later we met for lunch and I was so happy she gladly accepted. Dee immediately embraced the vision God had given me for the cover. She saw it in her heart and mind. God had confirmed to her she was the one to paint the tunnel and write her testimony. I really cannot imagine anyone else doing it. Let me introduce you to my dear friend Dee Keller and her heart—

AMY BIRCHFIELD

Dee's Heart:

I think what drives someone to want to draw or paint is seeing something beautiful or inspiring and wanting to save that moment in time. But the clock keeps ticking and the world keeps moving to the next hours, days, months, and years— those very special glimpses into the beauty of life just won't stand still. Facebook and Instagram are so popular now for that very reason. We want to capture and hold onto life.

A couple of years ago on Father's Day we gathered at our house to celebrate the dads in our family. Our grandson Jesse became a dad the year before and gave us this amazing little boy, Maddox, our first great-grandchild. As we were going around the table giving cards and gifts to each father, I heard two little voices call out to me from the plastic wading pool on the deck, "Mémère, come watch us."

I kept saying "Just a minute, girls. We're giving the daddies their gifts!" And then it was as if my eyes were just opened to see that the greatest gifts to the dads were the two little girls crying out for a little bit of our time so they could give us that which we long for the most— love. (I know they do that for attention too.) But isn't that what we want also? I did go outside and put my feet in the pool, and looked into their eyes and felt that welling up inside of myself that always brings tears of deep joy, longing, fulfillment, and pride.

As I looked at them, and through the window to the table where the family was sitting, I experienced one of those revealing moments when I knew that "I GOT IT!"

In the next moment little hands were holding my feet, washing them in swimming pool water, and I cried. (I'm crying now because I'm remembering.) The next thing I knew, the newest little boy was in the pool, with his daddy holding onto him, and Jesse's eyes locked onto mine for just a second, and again that swelling up of emotions filled my heart.

I vowed at that moment that I would not miss any more of those windows to heaven. Then I looked back at Jesse, and I saw it— that look of a father's love, a mother's love, a grandmother's love— and wondered if he was aware now, maybe for the first time, of how much *we love him*! "Oh, God, please reveal that to him now," I thought.

Reveal it to us also when we get so wrapped up in the unimportant that we miss the moments when *YOU* are in the room, waiting for us to notice *YOUR* amazing love.

It's been almost four months since my husband, Gene Keller, left this earth for heaven. I still have not fully realized that he is gone. My heart is still joined to his in some beautiful, painful, spiritual way. But at the same time, I am very aware that he is not here to hold my hand, to hold me, to talk to me, or like most of the time, to listen to me!

He was my problem solver, my strong shoulder, the only one here on earth who knew me— really knew me— and loved me anyway. He was the one I expected to be home when I got there, the one who looked for me when I was lost. He was the one who held my hand in the emergency room when I was sick or when he was sick. He was the one who led our devotions and prayers together in the mornings.

He reminded me that God was in control when I was fearful. He expressed his love for God when he sang, and always got choked up when he prayed.

But life has a way of continuing on even though it feels like it shouldn't. Since Gene left, we have celebrated Mother's Day, Father's Day, two anniversaries, and three family birthdays, including his. Our oldest grandson got married and our third great-grandchild, Lacie Mae, was born.

There are days when I don't cry at all, and some days I cry a lot. But most of the time I cry when I don't expect it.

I can tell you this much—from the moment they told me he was gone until right now, the Lord has carried me. In the middle of this terrible grief, I have experienced "peace" and the most unexpected moments of "joy."

During the memorial service we had at church, we sang some of the old gospel songs Gene loved to sing, and when we did, I felt a joy welling up inside of me that I could hardly contain. And I thought how is it possible to feel such sorrow and joy at the same time?

I wondered if this was what the Bible meant when it said "joy unspeakable and full of glory." I know for sure that the Lord lives and we will be with Him one day, but in those moments heaven came to earth and we were celebrating together.

Gene is home where he belongs now, but my story isn't over yet. He didn't leave me all at once, but each time I do some simple thing without him that we used to do together, I let go once more. Every memory hurts, but it also brings laughter as I relive a precious time with him. The sadness reminds me that he is not here anymore, but the joy tells me that those memories are mine, anytime I want to think of them. And when I share them with others, Gene is with us, smiling too.

But I have to be willing to hurt, to have the joy. They both come from deep inside and they never come alone.

As I look back on the last forty-nine years, I can see that God traveled through our lives, revealing Himself to us every day in some way. I wish I could paint you a picture of how it was. But God is still working on our story. It goes on in my life, and my children's lives, and so on, the people Gene touched, and the people they touched. Every time I tell my story, it has the potential of changing someone else's life, because God uses each of us to pass His love on. As an artist I can only try to paint what God has created, but He's the only one who can make life beautiful.

"Thank you, Lord, for the beauty You brought into my life with Gene, our children and theirs, and all the people who are part of our story. And thank You for the life You have planned now for me and the rest of my story."

And how blessed all those in whom You live, whose lives become roads You travel; They wind through lonesome valleys, come upon brooks, discover cool springs and pools brimming with rain! God-traveled, these roads curve up the mountain, and at the last turn—Zion!

God in full view!

Psalms 84:5-7 (The Message)
Dee Keller, Artist

Gene and Dee Keller

Acknowledgements

Richard S. Pierce, Dad, You encouraged me along the way. I so appreciate the time we spent at the dining room table. Your writing skills helped me improve greatly.

Johnita K. Pierce, Mom, You read my book or allowed me to read to you as I journeyed through. You are always my number one encourager. Thank you for your prayers and love.

Angela Farnell, my sister-in-love, Thank you for using your English grammar skills to proof read and edit my book on its first go around. You were so very encouraging on my journey.

Dee Keller, my dear friend, for painting the most beautiful and perfect artwork for the cover, I thank you. You absolutely received the vision God gave me for this book.

Tammy Melton, I thank you so very much for your encouragement and prayers. You truly are a gift from God.

Scott Birchfield, Thank you for your constant love and encouragement through the journey of writing this book and sharing my story. I love you!

Pamela Cherry, I treasure your friendship and I am eternally thankful for you introducing me to Captain Raymon George

Joining our lives as one

Captain Raymon & Mrs. Amy George
On our wedding day

PROLOGUE

My Princess Story

It was a beautiful sunny day on May 29, 1999. I didn't get much sleep during the night because I was so excited. It was my wedding day! I heard the birds singing outside my room all night long. It was as if they were celebrating and sharing in my happiness.

After a morning of preparing to be the beautiful bride for Raymon, I and my matron of honor Karen arrived at the Fort Eustis Chapel. I knew my captain was somewhere in the chapel getting ready in his dress blues. I could not wait to see him at the end of the red-carpeted center aisle.

I was so excited! I was surrounded by people I loved and my new army family. They made sure I knew I was joining a whole new world. I would be one of them. I smiled with great joy as I was escorted toward my handsome Captain by my dad to "Jesu, Joy of Man's Desiring" Bach. I looked to my left and saw my granny's smile. This moment was so very special to me.

My granny had been a career military wife and now she was watching her granddaughter follow in her footsteps. Granddad and Granny Hendley had been married for fifty-six years until Granddad had gone home to Heaven just two months earlier. She was so strong. I was so happy to see her as I walked down the aisle.

Granddad and Granny Hendley prepared me for my life in the military

I leaned over to give my mom a beautiful handkerchief with roses embroidered on it, I kissed her on her cheek, and I stepped forward to marry my prince.

My sweet Raymon was awaiting my arrival with a smile and a wink. Our beautiful ceremony began. We said our vows we personally had written and exchanged rings. We lit our unity candle and signed our marriage covenant.

My friend Jennifer read the words to the song "Make Us One" and quoted I Corinthians 13. (We had our wedding bands engraved with this beautiful reference.) Raymon was the first man with which I had ever experienced this kind of love.

> If I speak in the tongues of men or of angels, but do not have love, I am only a resounding gong or a clanging cymbal. ² If I have the gift of prophecy and can fathom all mysteries and all knowledge, and if I have a faith that can move mountains, but do not have love, I am nothing. ³ If I give all I possess to the poor and give over my body to hardship that I may boast, but do not have love, I gain nothing.
>
> ⁴ Love is patient, love is kind. It does not envy, it does not boast, it is not proud. ⁵ It does not dishonor others, it is not self-seeking, it is not easily angered, it keeps no record of wrongs. ⁶ Love does not delight in evil but rejoices with the truth. ⁷ It always protects, always trusts, always hopes, always perseveres.
>
> ⁸ Love never fails. But where there are prophecies, they will cease; where there are tongues, they will be stilled; where there is knowledge, it will pass away. ⁹ For we know in part and we prophesy

> in part, ¹⁰ but when completeness comes, what is in part disappears. ¹¹ When I was a child, I talked like a child, I thought like a child, I reasoned like a child. When I became a man, I put the ways of childhood behind me. ¹² For now we see only a reflection as in a mirror; then we shall see face to face. Now I know in part; then I shall know fully, even as I am fully known.
>
> ¹³ And now these three remain: faith, hope and love. But the greatest of these is love.
>
> I Corinthians 13 (NIV)

The Chaplain pronounced us as husband and wife and then he turned to me to give the signal I could begin my surprise to Raymon. I read the words of Shania Twain's song "From This Moment On." These lyrics articulated so well the words of my heart.

What a special moment it was when Raymon kissed me as his wife for the first time, and we were introduced as Captain and Mrs. George. "Trumpet Voluntary" began to play on the beautiful pipe organ. I placed my arm in my prince's arm and was escorted up the center aisle to start our new life together.

We hugged everyone on their way out the door as they lined up to blow their bubbles of congratulations.

We exited the chapel and entered through the drawn swords held by the Army's finest men and women. When we got to the last two swords, they were lowered in front of us to stop us from continuing to walk. We obliged the soldiers with a special kiss. Our guests cheered with joy. The swords were raised and we continued to walk. Surprisingly, a soldier swatted me in the butt quite hard with his sword, as is the military custom— I found out later. My journey as an Army wife had begun.

We took off in a limousine to go to our reception at the Omni Hotel. We toasted with a bottle of sparkling grape juice. I was excited to start our beautiful reception. We had a series of formal pictures taken and finally were able to eat.

Our DJ had asked us to prepare a love letter to share with each other. My letter had been written that morning while I sat in the salon chair preparing to get my hair fixed. With all of the preparation, I almost forgot. He took our letters and began to read Raymon's letter to me. It was so very sweet and loving. I could hear his mother in the background saying, "That is not my son!" She could not believe these sweet words were coming from him due to his well-known introverted nature. He was not one to share his deep feelings. Knowing this myself, Raymon's love letter meant so much to me. Next, the DJ read my letter to Raymon. It was so easy to express my love and appreciation to him.

It was time for our first dance. We danced to "The Power of Love" by Celine Dion followed by "My Special Angel" (Raymon's surprise dedication song to me). We danced while Raymon sang every word of the song. It was so sweet. I had never really heard it before. It was in Raymon's favorite style, fifties music. I dedicated the song "Because You Loved Me" by Celine Dion to Raymon. I felt in my heart of hearts this song clearly said what I felt about Raymon in my life.

We had such a good time dancing with our family and friends. We then said goodbye and started for the beginning of our honeymoon in a suite at the same hotel.

The next morning our Ford Explorer greeted us with many messages written all over the windows by our very special wedding party. We then began to travel to what was an unknown location for me. Raymon had full control of the whereabouts of our honeymoon.

We began our drive down the highway headed south. Our destination became clearer as we reached a beach road in North Carolina. I knew then we would be staying at a hotel on the beach. I was so excited. The places on the beach were to our left, but somehow we turned into a driveway on our right. There they were: two full-size army tanks. We entered into Fort Fisher, an Air Force recreational facility. He had rented a cabin for us. I wish I could say I was very gracious, but I did share my disappointment.

I would be spending the start of our honeymoon in a cabin with other families and couples. With great relief and happiness, we ended up having the times of our lives.

Everyone went home the next day because Memorial Day weekend was over. We had the cabin to ourselves. In a separate building just several feet away was a room with a private hot tub, a game area that included our favorite table game, Ping-Pong, and a gym. We ate at the best seafood restaurants where they had the best hush puppies.

We had our favorite dessert, ice cream, at this amazing custard place a few times throughout the week. We walked on the beach and a fantastic pier. It all ended up being wonderful!

We traveled home to Williamsburg, Virginia. We opened so many wonderful gifts from our family and friends. I started arranging beautiful things throughout his Star Trek bachelor pad. You should have seen this beautiful cherry display case. One shelf had flowers on it from the wedding, and the next shelf had Star Trek plates and so on.

Shortly after we arrived home and got settled, we attended our first military ball as husband and wife. This ball was to celebrate the Army's birthday on June 14, 1999. On our first date Raymon had invited me to this same ball, and it became an ongoing joke that I dated him for this perk. I have to say this is not the reason I entered into a relationship with him, but it sure was a nice bonus. I loved getting dressed up in my long evening gowns and getting my hair put up in all the different up-do hair-styles.

Raymon would get dressed in his dress blues with all of his impressive bars and awards on his chest. I felt like a true princess on the arm of my prince. I loved all the formalities and the dancing. It was such a highlight.

The following month we attended the Aviation Ball that was held at the Virginia Air & Space Center in Hampton, Virginia. Raymon was an aviator and he flew Hueys and Black Hawks. He loved flying and I loved seeing him in his flight suit. I never in a million years thought I would be married to a pilot. He was indeed my Officer and a Gentleman.

I had no idea what our adventure would behold, and I am so thankful God took us step by step into our future. This is our story.

Beginning our journey as Captain and Mrs. George

Beginning our journey as Captain and Mrs. George

CHAPTER I

An Army of One

Fort Rucker, Alabama

Our first military move was to Fort Rucker, Alabama in November 1999. This new town was a huge culture shock for me. I grew up surrounded by beautiful water and just about anything you wanted to do with several choices for any given activity. Enterprise, Alabama is a very small city, and in the center of their town square stands a beautiful lady statue holding up the Boll Weevil bug. I think this statue represents this city well.

Raymon and I rented a nice two-bedroom town home. Our real estate company gave me not only a place to live but also a place to work. I was their receptionist and placed in charge of their storage unit.

Six months later, we moved the trailer we thought we had sold back in Williamsburg onto Tiara Park, the trailer park on post. After a year there, we traded it in for a double-wide manufactured home on land. This is where we lived when September 11, 2001 changed all of our lives.

That morning Raymon had gone into work and I was resting before I started my day. Raymon called and told me to turn on the TV. I could not believe my eyes. When I started to watch the news, only the first plane had struck the first tower. I stood there and watched behind the news reporter as the second plane crashed into the next tower. This is when all of us knew this was not an accident but a terrorist attack.

I was due to be with my military sisters at the chapel for our Tuesday morning meeting. When I arrived, we all had to sign a sheet indicating that we were in attendance. It was a security procedure, one of many such procedures that began in our nation because of the terrorists that invaded our country.

During the meeting, the chaplain reported that both towers had crashed to the ground. We sat paralyzed in shock and tears. We could not believe this day. We also knew as military wives our personal lives would most likely be changed forever. Our husbands were soldiers.

The following year in November at a different chapel, Raymon had his pinning ceremony for his new rank as major. I stood beside him and assisted him in placing his first major pin on his shoulder. As his lieutenant colonel spoke serious words of what would be required of him in the next rank, I felt an ache in my heart. I didn't quite know why I felt this ache, but I knew with Raymon continuing on in the Army at this serious time there was a great chance he would have to face war. Raymon had the opportunity to retire after his twenty years of service, but he decided to continue with the rank of major.

We attended a marriage enrichment seminar on a weekend shortly after this ceremony. The seminar was sponsored by the Chaplain Corps, and the guest speaker gave us an assignment to take our large index cards and draw a picture illustrating our spouse.

Raymon was not one to really share his deepest feelings. Sometimes I wondered how he felt about me even though I knew he loved me. I will never forget how he stood up and held up his picture of a bright sun and some darkness. He said his life was very dark before he met me, and when I entered into his life, it was as if the sun shone brightly. He shared that I continued to be a great light in his life. My heart smiled and I was so overjoyed that my husband felt this way about me.

Raymon meant so much to me throughout our marriage. He was my hero in so many ways. He was really the one who believed in me through it all.

From the very beginning, Raymon would say that he could see me having a ministry like Joyce Meyer's. I had no thought of being in full-time ministry whatsoever. I would just pat him on the arm and say, "That is sweet, Honey." I knew in my heart there was no way that could be true. In fact, I shared the sweet thing Raymon said to me to our Sunday school class the following Sunday.

I sincerely waited for them all to break out in laughter. They did not. They just looked at me very seriously and said they could see it. That was definitely not the reaction I was looking for. I really thought I was an utter mess. I certainly didn't fit the bill to be a full-time minister, especially one like Joyce Meyer.

Raymon's belief in me was so very strong. He always invited me to every function he attended as an officer. In the Army, there are a lot of functions and dinners. The motto for the Army at that time was "An Army of One." We both took that seriously in our marriage.

The last week in January 2003 we received our next set of orders. We were headed to Germany. I was not excited about this because the war was raging in the Middle East and I wanted to stay in *my* country and in *my* comfort zone. I wrestled with this news for a while until February 9 when I was sitting in a Sunday night church service. This is when God spoke to my heart all night. He said to me, *Amy, Raymon received his orders the last week of January but tonight I am giving you My orders. You are going to serve Me with a specific role to fulfill.* I said, "Yes, Sir."

That night the youth pastor spoke on Matthew 19 in the Bible and shared with us about the rich man who asked Jesus what he had to do to serve Him. Jesus said, "Go and sell everything you have." The youth pastor said that Jesus was calling him out of his comfort zone and if we really want to see the glory of God in our lives, we must be willing to leave our comfort zone. You can't be more direct than that.

On March 19, sitting on our couch holding hands, Raymon and I watched the initial strike on Iraq. I knew down deep in the pit of my stomach this war was going to have a personal impact on us one day.

This day came way too soon. The following month when I returned home from a ladies retreat with my military sisters, Raymon sat me down and gave me the news. He had orders to join the First Armored Division in Iraq once we landed in Germany. The day that I knew was coming had arrived. I cried, scared to think that my sweet husband and best friend was going into a very dangerous situation.

During the next meeting I had with my sisters at chapel, I tried to share that my husband was going to war, but I could not get it out. The tears were coming so hard. A friend had to take my place in sharing the news. They were supportive, and at the same time I knew they were dreading what was to come for them. We enjoyed our last couple of months in Alabama. This huge move required a lot of preparation. My family and friends wondered why I was still going to Germany knowing that Raymon would be with me for just a month before his tour. I was confident I had my personal orders to go.

In Enterprise, there is a tall water tower that says "Enterprise, City of Progress." I would always giggle when I saw it because I had a personal opinion that would contradict this motto. God spoke to my heart and said, *Amy, this city was your city of progress in Me, and it will prepare you for what I have for you in the next assignment.*

While stationed at Fort Rucker, I did teach a couple of Bible studies. I was on the board for PWOC, (Protestant Women of the Chapel). I planned and led a spring ladies retreat and I was on the praise and worship team. God was grooming me for what I had never imagined would be in store for my future assignment.

<u>Wiesbaden, Germany</u>

On June 26, 2003, Raymon and I were excited to be leaving Enterprise, Alabama. We headed to the airport where we got on my first flight over the ocean. When we arrived, we were driven immediately to Hanau, Germany. I think we were there maybe an hour when Raymon got the call that we would be staying there only for the weekend. This was the military way. Raymon would always say, "Be fluid because being flexible is too rigid." This was so true in living out the military life.

On Monday, a lieutenant picked us up and drove us about forty-five minutes to our new city, Wiesbaden, Germany. We stayed in the American hotel where most soldiers and their families make their transition into their new quarters or prepare to leave to go back home.

We met a wonderful couple that was also facing the same future as we were. We would walk down the block and have dinner together in the evenings. During the days, a bus would take us onto the post to complete our processing responsibilities. The first time we took the bus onto the post, it was a very scary experience. The bus driver asked us to have our ID cards out and ready for the German soldiers to see. When the German soldier came onto the bus with his machine gun around his neck, I knew I was no longer in Kansas.

We sat through many briefings to inform us about our new life in Germany. One of the talks had to do with not dressing in patriotic clothes. We were asked for our own safety not to stand out as Americans. This was going to be a very adventurous stay in this new country.

Raymon had a long list of departments we were required to visit. One of these departments was the Family Readiness Group or FRG office. This was the office responsible for the families of the First Armored Division.

When we met the army liaison for this office and talked with her about our status of being apart in a month, she looked at me and asked, "Do you want to be our FRG Leader?" I looked at her with an "Are you serious?" look. First, I had never been in a Family Readiness Group, and second, I thought this would be a role for a general's wife. I told her, "I will think about it."

Later while sitting at the food court, Raymon and I watched President Bush giving a speech on TV. In his speech, he was talking about the importance of an FRG Leader and what an important role she had to play. First of all, I could not believe my ears, but suddenly I felt as if God were nudging me. So I prayed a prayer that if the FRG Leader role was still available, I would accept the position.

A week later I stopped by the FRG office. I walked in practically holding my breath and asked if they had filled the president's position.

The liaison said, "Yes."

For a second I felt relief, and then she finished by saying, "You." That day it was decided I was the official FRG Leader of the First Armored Division. I would have my own office on post and I would work full-time hours as a volunteer. God had indeed given me my orders, and I found out very quickly what they were.

Raymon and I moved into our new home two days before he was scheduled to leave for Iraq. The movers came the next day with all the boxes. A lot of wives were slave-driving their husbands to get their homes in order before they left. I felt that I had all year to unpack boxes and make ours a home. I just wanted to spend as much quality time as we could together.

Raymon tried to keep a positive outlook on his tour. "I'm looking forward to putting all my training into practice," he would say. Raymon had been involved in other serious situations, but this was the first war he was deployed into.

On our last night together, Raymon isolated himself in the room to pack all of his gear. We exchanged gifts for our monthly wedding anniversary. We had celebrated every month in some special way since we were married. I gave him a book of beautiful, colorful views around the world. I felt it might help since he would be surrounded by desert. He didn't want to ruin it so he left it with me.

Because we did not have our Mazda Tribute yet, our sweet friends we had met in the hotel took us to the post for this awful, dreaded, in- the-middle-of-the-night farewell.

It was so sad to watch other soldiers say goodbye to their spouses, and then it was our turn. Raymon said, "Goodbye. I'll see you in nine months." We hugged, and he got on the bus.

This was the hardest thing I had ever had to face at that point in my life. I actually felt a tie to my heart being pulled out of my chest as the bus drove away. I was in incredible pain. My heart hurt so badly.

The rear detachment lieutenant tried to talk to me casually, as though what had just happened was business as usual. I was thinking to myself, *Does this guy see the anguish I am in?* I politely let him know I was not in the mood to talk small talk or military business. He was trying to tell me it was all going to be fine. I thought to myself, *Do you realize those soldiers, my husband, are off to war?* I cried all the way home and my friend walked me up to my apartment. She hugged me and assured me she was just a sidewalk away.

I called my mom, whose time zone was six hours behind mine. My dad, mom, and sister were fully awake. My sister, Dawn, answered the phone. I wanted somehow for them to help with the pain but I knew nothing could. I crawled into the bed and just wept.

I was so tired the next day. All I wanted to do was stay in bed. The phone rang, and it was the FRG liaison. She asked me to please come to the headquarters because the rear detachment commander wanted to meet me. Again, it was the military way: stop crying and march on! We have work to do.

I went into the headquarters building looking, I am sure, like a mess. The commander began to tell me what he expected from the FRG Leader. I assured him that I was ready and up for the task. I apologized for how I looked. I explained my husband left in the middle of the night. He told me he knew because he was the one who sent him. I have to say the whole situation with the commander bringing me in and talking to me was quite interesting. It was as if they knew I was in my bed depressed from it all.

God blessed me immediately upon my arrival into my new home. He placed me right next door to another military sister who also was from my beautiful home state of Virginia. Her husband was deployed a few months before our arrival in Germany. Terri was a pro at living in Germany, and she became such a dear friend. We were a support to one another. Often, she would make us coffee and ask me over. I could slip over in my comfy clothes because we were the only two that lived on the same floor of a three-story building.

When it came to communication between Raymon and me, we were given several different options. I was so very thankful for this blessing, especially knowing that soldiers from most of the previous wars and their spouses did not have this same privilege.

First, we had the military phone. One of the perks of having my own post office was having a military connection. Second, we communicated by e-mails and instant messaging. Third, and my favorite, was the recorded tapes we would send on a monthly basis. We each had a small recorder and mini cassettes. We were able to talk without the garbled sounds in the background of the phones. I also loved listening to his voice when I went to sleep at night in my bed. He sang his special song to me, "My Special Angel." He talked to me on his walk to his office telling me how much he missed me and how he could not wait to see me again. He told me how very proud he was of me for serving as the FRG Leader and talked about all the things we would do when he got back. I could not wait for that day.

I placed his Bible, opened to Psalm 91, in the window sill. I would lay my hand on it and pray nightly, word for word, these scriptures over Raymon. It gave me great peace to know I could trust God with my husband.

1Whoever dwells in the shelter of the Most High will rest in the shadow of the Almighty.

2I will say of the Lord, "He is my refuge and my fortress, my God, in whom I trust."
3Surely he will save you
from the fowler's snare
and from the deadly pestilence.
4He will cover you with his feathers,
and under his wings you will find refuge;
his faithfulness will be your shield and rampart.
5You will not fear the terror of night, nor the arrow that flies by day,
6 nor the pestilence that stalks in the darkness,
nor the plague that destroys at midday.
7A thousand may fall at your side, ten thousand at your right hand, but it will not come near you.
8You will only observe with your eyes and see the punishment of the wicked.
9If you say, "The Lord is my refuge," and you make the Most High your dwelling,
10 no harm will overtake you, no disaster will come near your tent.
11For he will command his angels concerning you to guard you in all your ways;

**12they will lift you up in their hands, so that you will not strike your foot against a stone.
13You will tread on the lion and the cobra;
you will trample the great lion and the serpent.
14"Because he loves me," says the Lord, "I will rescue him; I will protect him, for he acknowledges my name.
15He will call on me, and I will answer him;
I will be with him in trouble,
I will deliver him and honor him.
16With long life I will satisfy him and show him my salvation."**

Psalm 91 (NIV)

Raymon laying his hand on Psalm 91 the evening he returned home from Iraq

I sent him sweet messages. I told him I was so proud to be his wife and I missed him very much. I told him about things happening back in Germany. One thing I was determined to do for his whole tour in Iraq was to keep things positive. I knew he was in a terrible situation, and I was not going to add to his stress.

I got so mad at women who would get mad at their spouses over stupid stuff. One woman wrote her soldier a Dear John letter while he was in Iraq. He ended up committing suicide. I felt this woman was guilty of murder. Why in the world would you be so selfish as to complain or make your loved one miserable when they were already in a rotten situation?

Shortly after I started my role as Family Readiness Group Leader, one of the ladies came into the office and introduced herself. While we were talking, she mentioned Protestant Women of the Chapel. I shared with her that I was very involved with PWOC in Alabama. She informed me they were looking for a praise and worship leader. Next thing I knew, God had me take on this role. I was thinking, *Wow God, You were really serious when You said You had orders for me.*

The next month I served as the worship leader for the Protestant Chapel service at Hainerberg Chapel. This service was attended by an average of four hundred people. I served until we moved from Wiesbaden.

God indeed had orders for me to fulfill. It was a blessing to be placed in a position where my focus had to be on praise and worship to God while I was in the midst of war on my home front. This kept my head lifted to the source of all comfort and peace through the storm.

Raymon encouraged me before he left for Iraq to audition for a play at the American theater in Wiesbaden, the Amelia Earhart Playhouse. The audition was only a week after he left. I went and had no idea what would happen, but I wanted to make my husband happy. I ended up getting the lead in a delightful play called *The Blind Date*.

I enjoyed everything about it. I enjoyed all of the rehearsals, and I absolutely loved being on a live stage. I also received a write-up in the German newspaper.

My director was German, as was a fellow actress. They had to translate what the write-up said for me, and it was very good. I also was in two other plays. One of the plays received the European Topper Award for Community Theater throughout Europe for Best Comedy. I felt as if we had won a Tony award!

This was an exciting awards ceremony. I wished Raymon were there to see all of these amazing opportunities for me, especially since he was the one to encourage me to audition.

One of the greatest satisfactions I had as the FRG Leader was scheduling all of the family members to come to headquarters and see their spouses down range through a VTC (Video Tele Conference). These happened every Saturday, and each family received an opportunity each month. The time limit was an average of ten minutes each to accommodate each family. I would always be present because I knew this was the only way I could touch base with every family member. I would usher them into the board room, watch the time, and then have to do the not-so-fun job of telling them they had to leave.

I was also able to get a spot each month for myself. I loved to see Raymon on the big screen. Often he would be swatting at a bunch of mosquitoes trying to attack him, but our times together were very precious. I was so thankful for these VTCs. Can I just say how much I love technology?

For Christmas time, I came up with a special idea for the families. I decorated the board room with Christmas decorations and I informed the wives and husbands to bring wrapped gifts for the children. This way the soldiers could somehow be a part of seeing their children's Christmas. I could tell the families really enjoyed this special time no matter how short.

I was also responsible for creating monthly meetings for the families. Again for Christmas, we had a Santa Claus and I dressed up as Santa's helper. Each child came up to receive a present and get a picture for the parents. We had goodies for everyone to enjoy. My heart's mission was to ease the pain of this deployment for all of the families the best I could.

Speaking of Christmas, I went home to see my parents with another military spouse that also had family in the same area of Virginia. It felt so strange to go back to the United States without Raymon. My mom was amazing during my two week vacation at home. She arranged for me to do something special every single day.

For example, we went to Christmas parties, she took me to see a ballet, and we had special dinners out. I asked her to give me my schedule each day so that I would not feel overwhelmed. She really made it very special for me. Raymon surprised me with a call on Christmas. I really did not expect to be able to communicate with him but he made it happen. It was our first Christmas apart. I sent him a huge box of presents and things that I had hoped would make him happy before I left Germany.

I had a sheet of paper with rows of numbers representing the days left for Raymon to come home. It truly felt like a marathon and you do things like that to help you get through it all. I received a very difficult call in March letting me know that the soldiers would not be home the following month as scheduled but would be delayed another ninety days. When you feel that close to the finish line and someone moves it that far, it is devastating. I was so close to despair yet I looked up from my desk to see my door hanger that said "Hope". It looked like the word "Hope" was being highlighted from God. I knew He was encouraging me to keep trusting Him. He had everything under control.

Terri and I ended up traveling together from Mainz, Germany on a train to the Port of Rome to catch a Mediterranean cruise that was originally supposed to be my anniversary cruise with Raymon. I could not receive a refund so Terri was a true friend and traveled with me.

While Terri and I were on the cruise, I got a message from Raymon through e-mail that he would be home the day after I got back from the cruise for his two-week R & R (Rest and Relaxation).

Isn't that something? I cannot tell you how many times the military conflicted with my life's schedule. I could have taken this cruise with Raymon if I had only known. I have to say the excitement of Raymon being home overrode any feelings of frustration. He was coming home on June 2, 2004.

I will always remember that day. After I made sure I looked amazing, I arrived at the airport. I parked and went inside but could not find him. I ran into an airport employee who directed me to another building. I got into my car and drove over to the suggested building and parked.

This time I ran into another wife who was in the same boat I was in. We could not find our husbands, and both of us found our adrenaline pumping.

It was nice to know I was not alone in that moment. Our husbands were the very last on the R & R rotation out of Iraq due to their late arrival into Iraq. It had been ten months since I had seen Raymon. We ran into a man in the building who quickly exclaimed,

"Both of your husbands are waiting for you in front of the airport. I just dropped them off."

We ran out of the building, dismissed the notion of taking our cars, and walked quickly to the front of the airport. I felt as if I were walking on clouds. I don't think my feet touched the ground. All of a sudden, I saw two men, and one of them raised a Mountain Dew bottle up in the air. I knew immediately it was him because Mountain Dew was Raymon's favorite drink. We embraced and I could not let him go. I did not care about all the people who were around, either. I was just so happy to have him back in my arms.

We had an amazing two weeks together. We acted more like newlyweds than when we were actually newlyweds. I was so happy to have him with me.

The very sad day came when I had to drive him back to the airport to return to Iraq. He scrunched over, saying his stomach was aching. He did not want to return, even for a month. I knew it was horrific when I saw him acting like this. He was so strong all the time, and his favorite motto was, "If it doesn't kill you, it makes you stronger." He said this long before Kelly Clarkson's song, which always makes me think back of him and his saying.

I began to play Josh Groban's "You Raise Me Up" on the CD player. I felt this was the perfect moment to play a song that would communicate my deep gratitude and respect for him. I so wanted him to know how very proud I was of him and try to encourage him to face the war once again. He appreciated it and it seemed to give him some peace. We finally arrived at his reporting station. It had been such a difficult drive. I sat with him in the car for a moment until he said he had to go. I could tell he had put on his "major's hat."

I just kept telling myself that he would be home in a month. It felt like the longest month I have ever experienced. During this month, I was helping reunite families with their soldiers. The first soldiers who entered Iraq were the ones who came home first. Our first welcome home celebration was really special. We had only thirty soldiers to reunite so it was quite different from the rest. We lined up the soldiers at one end of a hallway and had their families lined up in order on the opposite end. As each soldier's name was called, he or she would walk forward, and the families ran to meet them. It was amazing to see these families back together.

Over the course of the month, we reunited several more troops and families in the hangar. Finally it was our day—July 11, 2004. It was on a Sunday and it was the most exciting day! We gathered together in the huge hangar around 5:30 p.m. The time was creeping by. I sang a solo, "God Bless the USA" by Lee Greenwood, followed by a female soldier that sang the National Anthem. We knew they were lined up and ready to march in.

The large hangar door lifted up as they were marching forward in their formation. My heart was beating so hard and fast. My friend said she would take pictures since her husband had already returned. I looked for Raymon, but it was so hard because frankly they looked a lot alike in their uniforms. Finally, I got a glimpse of him, but of course he couldn't wave to me. The commander was merciful because he said very few words, and then came the words we all were waiting for, "Fall Out." The families all hurried off the bleachers and raced to their soldier. I was having a hard time at first, and then I found him. He handed me a rose, and then we just held each other. I was so glad it was finally over. The war was over!

Raymon returned home from war on July 11, 2004.

Raymon was not home for very long when I realized the war was not over at all. Raymon was having nightly PTSD (Post Traumatic Stress Disorder) episodes ranging from three to five a night— every night. He would scream as if he were being held over a lake of fire and about to be dropped. Every scream was crying out for "Jesus!" I had no idea what to do except just try to comfort him. I had never seen anything like this before. The war was no longer just in Iraq. It was inside our home.

Now that my FRG leadership role was over, I started working at the credit union on post. I worked full-time hours, and I really enjoyed working with our members very much. It was also nice to do something I enjoyed and receive a paycheck. The FRG had chosen to rearrange things, and frankly I was very happy about it. I was battle weary.

At a division dinner we attended, I received an honor that was very unexpected. The commanding general of the First Armored Division, General Martin Dempsey, and who currently serves as the Chairman of the Joints Chief of Staff said a few words and the next thing I knew he called my name.

I came forward and he placed a medal around my neck. It was the Heart of Victory Medal and was given for my work throughout the year for the FRG. I could tell Raymon was so proud of me. It really made me happy to make my husband, whom I respected highly, feel proud of me and my service to his division.

The nightmares continued. I would sleep soundly, and then suddenly Raymon would scream at the top of his lungs. It seemed as if I jumped clear up in the air. This would happen over and over every night. We lived a total of a year together in Wiesbaden before our next duty station move.

Before we moved, we took a tour to London, England to celebrate our sixth anniversary on May 29, 2005. We traveled with a popular tour company that dealt a lot with military families. When the bus picked us up at the front of the post, lo and behold, our sweet friends that we met back at the beginning in the American hotel were sitting on the bus. This was such a great surprise, and talk about a full-circle experience. We enjoyed the tour together, and we were able to catch up on all the details we had missed not seeing one another.

Our hotel sat right next to Heathrow Airport, and it was fun looking out our sound-proof glass window as the big jets flew in for the landing. I have always loved watching airplanes since I was very young, as I grew up in a house that was in the flight pattern of our busy local airport.

We rode the Tube into the main part of the city. We went to see the show *Chitty Chitty Bang Bang* on the London Theater strip. We also toured Madame Tussauds, the very famous wax museum. We visited Buckingham Palace at the perfect moment, arriving just in time for the Changing of the Guard. They marched down the street just as I have seen them do on TV so many times before. We enjoyed our time away very much.

Our actual anniversary was the day we rode back to Germany. Raymon was so quiet. We actually sat in two different rows of seats. I could tell he did not want to be bothered. It may have been all the togetherness we had just experienced over the weekend or something much deeper within.

Mannheim, Germany

We moved to Mannheim, Germany shortly after our trip to England. We went from living in a stairwell apartment to a townhome with four bedrooms and three bathrooms. It was really a fantastic place for military housing. Raymon and I decided that for my well-being I should have my own bedroom.

I had never wanted that type of situation between my husband and me, but frankly, after a year of his nightmares I needed a break, especially with working full time. I started working at another credit union in Heidelberg. I enjoyed the job and the people I worked with very much. A few months later, I was able to make a transfer within the same credit union right onto the post where we lived.

We enjoyed a beautiful bike path that was very close to our home. One thing I loved about Germany was the simplicity of life. Raymon would ride his bike down this path all the way to work most days. I believe it helped Raymon to have this therapeutic bike ride.

His episodes went down from the usual three to five to just one to three a night. He would continue

For I Know The Plans

to scream out for Jesus. He would scream, "Jesus, help me!"

I would listen, comfort, and then wonder why Jesus was not listening to his screams. This is the kind of circumstance that tries our faith. Will we continue to fight the good fight of faith when our circumstances scream at us not to believe? We either choose to have faith in Jesus or we don't. I am so glad I continued to trust Him. He was faithful through it all. He gave us strength to endure every day. A song that ministered to me during these difficult days was "Blessed Be Your Name" by Matt Redman. Throughout my journey, I continue to say no matter what, blessed be the name of the Lord!

When I lived in Wiesbaden, I informed God I did not want any responsibilities in ministry or anything that would build relationships in Mannheim. We had only one year remaining in our tour of Germany, and I did not want any close relationships.

One of the things I found in the military life is how you make dear friends and, before you know it, one of you has to move away. I didn't want to hurt anymore, so I was going to try to stay undercover.

I attended a PWOC conference while I was still in Wiesbaden. PWOC hosted a widespread European conference yearly. The seating arrangement in the conference hall had all of the ladies seated by the location of their chapter. When I noticed the Mannheim ladies seated near me, I went over to meet them. When I introduced myself, the president of their chapter said that my reputation had preceded me and they asked me on the spot if I would be their praise and worship leader. I just laughed inside, thinking that no matter what you plan, what God wants for you will always win out. God always knows what is best for us. I ended up loving the role I fulfilled in PWOC, and along with being the praise and worship leader I also served as a Bible study teacher. God put me in a place where I would focus on two major things that would help me through the battle we were facing: praise and worship and the word of God.

It was a very fulfilling year. Another great part of my year with PWOC was being a part of a great Beth Moore Bible study titled "Believing God." In the study we were given a blue ribbon to wear around our wrist. This ribbon was to signify our five proclamations:

- I believe God is who He says He is
- God can do what He says He can do
- I am who God says I am
- I can do what God says I can do
- God's word is alive and active in me

At the end of this Bible study, we were instructed to take off our blue ribbon and make it into a bookmark. I chose to keep my blue ribbon on. I wore it to tell myself and the enemy that no matter what I am going through, "I choose to believe God."

I attended a second European conference while living in Mannheim. At this conference, God showed me a glimpse of what Raymon had seen in me from the beginning.

We had a wonderful praise and worship leader for the whole conference. She had her own workshop one afternoon, and I attended and was blessed. I went forward to introduce myself and let her know how much I appreciated her and the gift she was sharing with us. I was happily surprised when she asked if I wanted to go down the block for some tea.

We walked down the block in the quaint German town. During our wonderful time conversing, I felt led to share the vision God had given me about my own ministry. I didn't have a name for it. I could only describe it. I wanted to work with churches all over the country to use performing arts to bring God's message. My heart's desire was to encourage the gifts and talents of individuals in doing this. She listened with great interest. I shared with her how God had given me music dramas to encourage the churches I had attended.

She surprised me when she asked if I would write and perform a music drama to a song she wrote for her concert, which would be held in the large conference hall in a couple of days. I said, "We can see if God gives me something." She didn't place any pressure on me. It would certainly have to be God to pull this off.

Frances played two of her songs on the piano when we got back to the conference hall. I really didn't get anything, and then she played the third song, "Love Me." God gave it to me! I had the outline for the drama.

God placed the right people in front of me, and I found all the costumes and props I needed. I knew God had indeed put it all together. I was four hours away from my home, and God met every need for this drama. We performed the music drama during her concert, and it was beautiful! Frances said, "I will never see this song the same way again." I asked her permission to use her music for future dramas and she said, "Yes." I bought several of her wonderful CDs and looked forward to seeing what God would have in store.

Not only did it bless the audience, but it also blessed each woman who played a role in the drama. God had placed each woman in a role that pertained to her life's situation. God was speaking and dealing with each one in a very personal way. God wanted them to know that it is not about their performance or their imperfections but only about loving Him.

A couple of days later, Raymon picked me up from the train station. When we arrived home, we sat in the driveway talking for an hour. He looked at me with his sweet smile and said, "You are starting to believe it." Raymon always had confidence in me and that God had a special plan for my life. He saw that I was starting to believe it too, and I was. My belief was so strong that I was inspired with the name of my future ministry-Beloved Freedom.

Our seven-year anniversary came on May 29, 2006. This time we were able to take a Mediterranean cruise together. We flew to Venice where the ship was docked. We were so happy to get on the ship to relax.

For I Know The Plans

It had been quite a tour in Germany. Our first port was Athens, Greece.

We decided to explore the city both on our own and with a cab driver we hired. The cab driver drove us to the very famous Parthenon. We decided not to go up to the structure but rather walk around the base of it.

An interesting thing happened while we were about to leave. A woman was selling tablecloths, and she would not let me leave without one. I turned her down several times, but she continued to persist. Finally her price was so low, I had to take it. What occurred to me later is that the tablecloth was made of cotton material, and that was the traditional anniversary gift for the eighth year. Raymon and I would celebrate eight years of marriage on our next anniversary.

Our taxi driver drove us to the original sight of the original Olympics and to where the Olympics were held in 2004. It was very exciting to see these places I never thought I would be able to see.

Our next port was Mykonos. We walked around the water and looked at the shops. We had such a relaxed attitude about everything we did. It was a nice escape from reality. We did not get off the ship again until it was time to get off in Venice. We were both tired and really wanted to rest. Overall, we had a wonderful cruise.

The year in Mannheim was drawing to a close, and so was our tour in Germany. We were going home to the land I love. You do not realize how much you miss the United States flag flying until you live out of country.

Our next orders were to Atlanta, Georgia. This city girl was moving to the big city, and I was so excited! Raymon would be working for First Army located on Fort Gillem. We were also very excited because we were on our way to buying a new home. I was so ready to have my space and my privacy. We did not have much of this while living in Germany.

Transition back to the U.S.A.

The day came for us to say goodbye to Germany. It was June 23, 2006. Before we started our new journey in Atlanta, we headed for our month-long vacation tour. First stop was Austin, Texas, where Raymon's family lived. A bonus for me was that my first morning back in the United States began with a breakfast date with two of my close girlfriends I was stationed with in Wiesbaden. We were all on the board for PWOC as well. They met me at the Denny's right next to the hotel, and it was a celebration and welcome home party!

After a nice visit with Raymon's family, we stayed at my friend Suzanne's house for a couple of days. She was stationed at Fort Hood at the time. Raymon and I were sleeping in adjoining rooms connected by a bathroom the first night that we were there. During the middle of the night I went to the bathroom, and all of a sudden, I heard Raymon scream out. I ran into the room he was staying in, and he was in a deep sweat. He also had the sheets clinched tightly in his hands. It was different than the other times.

I got a cool washcloth and tried my best to comfort him. I was so scared. The next day he didn't remember the incident, but he said he felt as if he had been hit by a tractor-trailer truck. He wanted to just relax while Suzanne and I went out for a little bit.

After we left Austin we flew to Newport News, Virginia to see my family. Whenever Raymon and I came home from Germany, our heads would be spinning with all of the things there were to enjoy.

I remember standing in front of a popular doughnut shop staring like a crazy woman at all of their doughnuts. The girl behind the counter was trying to keep from looking at me like I was weird. I tried to explain to her I had been living in Germany, and I really did not enjoy their pastries and desserts. She just nodded. It was really like being on a high.

Our next stop was Orlando. We had a timeshare there, and we were headed to enjoy all of Orlando. We asked my sister to join us. I believe this is when I became the third wheel.

Raymon and Dawn both enjoyed riding on anything that had a drop. I, on the other hand, am not a drop kind of woman. I was the coatrack and I would watch them enjoy themselves like two little kids. I have to say I was a little disappointed, but I was also happy to see Raymon have a great time.

They would appease me throughout the trip by riding on the carousel and other rides I enjoy. We watched as well. The night at Cinderella's Castle was a very special highlight because I surprised my sister with a very special dinner where she met Cinderella. She had wanted to meet her since she was five.

After my sister flew home, we had a very important reunion to attend. Raymon was going to see his dad. This was huge because Raymon and his dad were estranged from each other for many years. God had done a lot in Raymon's heart despite all that he had gone through. He called his dad several weeks before this reunion to tell him he wanted to have a relationship with him. Raymon forgave him for leaving his family and not having anything to do with them since Raymon was eight years old.

Standing there watching Raymon hug his dad for the first time in many years was so moving. We spent the whole weekend with Raymon's dad and his wife.

The first night, they took us to the Medieval Times dinner theater. I had never been to such an interesting and fun show like this before. Then we went to play miniature golf, where we had such a great time. The next day we ate out and came back to the hotel lobby to play cards all afternoon. I do not think I had ever seen Raymon talk so much in our entire time together. I knew this was so healing for him and his dad.

After we said goodbye to his dad and his wife, we went on a short cruise to recuperate before our final landing in Atlanta. We left out of Port Canaveral and sailed to Nassau. We slept often on the cruise. We were downright exhausted, and I am really glad we had this cruise to unwind. We had a lot of things we were headed for once we made it to Atlanta. While on the cruise, we sat right next to a family who lived in the area of Georgia we were planning to move to, the Fayetteville/ Peachtree City area. They were a very nice family, and it gave us something else to look forward to as we moved to Atlanta.

Fort Gillem, Georgia

We finally flew to our new city and home in Atlanta. We stayed for a month in a popular hotel located in Fayetteville, Georgia. We heard great things about this town, and it was fairly close to his post. If we were not on post getting processed in, we were being escorted around town by our realtor.

One day when we were going around post for processing, I told Raymon I wanted to check into their PWOC office and see about their national conference coming up in the fall. When I walked into the director of education's office, she was very nice but she looked at me in a very interesting way. After I introduced myself, she suddenly asked if I would be willing to be the president for their PWOC chapter at Fort

McPherson. I looked at Raymon and he was smiling that sweet smile. He was saying with his eyes, "I told you God has His hand on you for ministry."

What was so interesting was that I knew they should have had a President back in April. Here it was the very end of July.

She informed me that the slot was empty because the board felt in all of their hearts that they were supposed to wait. The Lord had told them to wait and that He was going to bring the president to them. She said that the moment I walked into the office, she knew it was me. I just sat there in a stunned blur. She also informed me that they were leaving the next day to go to the vice president's parents' house to have a mini board retreat and she would love for me to come. I looked over at Raymon and he said, "Go."

I left the next day with a group of ladies I had never met. We headed to the mountains of Georgia. God flooded my heart with such love for all of these ladies. I knew I was to inform them at lunch of my decision as we sat around the table. "I will be honored to accept the position of president." They were all excited, and they knew God had indeed answered their prayers. God does not waste any time. He surprised me with His plan when I moved to Germany, and now He was doing it when I landed in Georgia.

When I arrived home from my trip, I got a call from our realtor. She said she found the home. We met her in Fayetteville, and she was right. We both loved it! We could see ourselves living in this home. It had an open, hospitable layout, and we could see ourselves entertaining our friends and family in it. We signed on the dotted line on August 25, 2006.

Not long after we moved into our home, Raymon had something that seemed like a seizure during his sleep. This was different from any of the episodes before. I encouraged him to see a doctor. They could not find that anything was wrong. I just prayed that it would be an isolated event to be seen no more.

The following month, PWOC had their very own special Sunday service at the chapel. I was honored to give the message. I was given the choice to choose a suggested message or one of my own choice. I prayed about it, and I waited to see what God wanted me to do.

One night as I lay next to Raymon, God spoke to me about what He wanted me to share. It was about love. The Lord downloaded everything I needed for the message into my spirit. I just needed to write it all down and look up some of the references in the Bible and I was set. I was thrilled that I heard from the Lord and it was settled!

The Sunday morning message was on love. Our role as Christians on this earth is to love. I was able to give them some practical ways of how to do this. This message was good and encouraged me. We are to love everyone we come in contact with. This is how people know we are Christians, and not only that, but also this is what our purpose in life is: to love. We are made in the image of God, and our life's bottom-line mission is to love one another.

After the service, Raymon and I stood at the back of the chapel shaking people's hands. I was very encouraged by everyone. They shared with me how the message inspired them, and some even said they hadn't heard such a powerful message like that in a long time. I give all credit to my Daddy God.

In November, things went from bad to worse for Raymon. It happened on his first day of work after the long Veterans Day weekend. Raymon called me to ask when he should request leave for the Thanksgiving break. I did not know. I told him we would discuss it further. To be honest, I was having an attitude and I was short with him. Then I got a call about two hours later that I never saw coming.

Raymon called to inform me he had had a daytime episode. He was reading a poem about a soldier on his computer, and the next thing he knew he was sitting in his chair surrounded by several fellow soldiers staring at him with great concern.

I felt as if I had just been punched in the gut. This could not be happening. We had dealt with this privately for so long, and now it was out in the open. Not only that, but also I thought Raymon was progressively getting better as time away from the war marched on. I suddenly was being dropped down the longest rollercoaster in my life. This had been our private battle, and now it was public and out of our hands.

The military started demanding that Raymon see other doctors, and it became very stressful.

The roller-coaster ride continued for both of us. We felt we were in a constant up-and-down emotional and mental ride. Raymon, through everything with PTSD, was so wonderful to me.

A lot of times when you hear someone is dealing with PTSD, anger is associated with it somehow. The whole time we were together, Raymon raised his voice to me maybe five times. He was always committed to not ever taking out his frustration on me, and I so appreciated that.

I tried to ease his frustration and pain through this very stressful time. Whenever he asked if he had had an episode in the night, I would say, "Raymon, if you don't remember it, then let it be." I just wanted his reality to be free from these nightmares and episodes. We dealt with daytime episodes and seizure activity for the next several months. Raymon was no longer allowed to drive to work. Thankfully, he had a kind-hearted coworker who gave him daily rides. It was a very stressful time, and I took on the role of protector and comforter. There were many uncertainties in our lives.

I was even noticing some Secondary Post Traumatic symptoms in me. I was always feeling on edge because I didn't know when the next episode or seizure would happen. I simply tried to make the best of our lives amid such chaos. I even enrolled us in square dancing classes.

One of my favorite memories from our class was one time when we were on break from learning our routines. They played "Achy Breaky Heart" by Billy Ray Cyrus, and out came my quiet, reserved Raymon running out in the middle of the room. He started shaking his booty, and I just had to follow after him. We gave everyone a great show with our dancing routine. We had a blast! Everyone was clapping and laughing, and it was a very special time.

We were very happy in February because Raymon had no seizures, night episodes, or day episodes. I just knew God was healing him finally. Raymon had so much energy, and his face was beaming. Our friends would even comment about how his face was majestic looking. I was so very thankful. I felt like I was getting my healthy Raymon back.

Raymon's birthday was February 26, and it was on a Monday. Raymon went to work, and I started preparing a very special evening. We had spent the whole weekend celebrating Raymon's birthday with friends, but tonight it was just the two of us. We enjoyed each other's company very much.

I bought Scooby Doo hanging decorations because Raymon loved Scooby Doo. I bought the party supply shop's very last balloon of the Indianapolis Colts, a leftover from the Super Bowl. Raymon was from Indiana and was a Colts fan. I was so happy they won the Super Bowl that year. I wanted to spoil my man for his birthday, so I bought all kinds of gifts. He deserved it all and much more.

One thing he was really going to be surprised about was one of those rubber change-holders that you bend open. He loved his old one he had for many years, and he couldn't find a new one. I found it! I also bought his newly issued army uniform and all the patches that he needed.

The dining room area was decorated with all of his favorite things, his oldies music was playing in the background, and I looked beautiful for him. I was excited and ready for him to walk through the door. He was surprised!

Before we enjoyed our evening at home, we had dinner at one of our favorite steak restaurants. One of their birthday traditions is that after they sing the birthday song, the birthday person has to kiss this big ole moose. Raymon did. When we got home, I presented Raymon with a pan of delicious brownies with nuts topped with chocolate frosting. It was a favorite of his. I placed the "4" and the "3" candles on top. He stood over his "birthday cake," made a wish, and blew out the candles. I wondered what the wish was, but he never revealed his secret wish.

We enjoyed the brownies, and then it was time for Raymon to open up his presents. I don't know who was more excited. He opened up each one and was very thankful for it all.

We then went upstairs to fix up his new uniform. Raymon put on his uniform, and I placed each patch on. It was a very special time, because we talked about each patch and what it symbolized. Finally, he was ready for the next day and I took a picture. He looked so good. We enjoyed the rest of the evening together.

The next night was our Tuesday square dance lesson night, but first we enjoyed dinner at our favorite fast-food restaurant. At dinner, we were talking about my trip to Newport News the next day. I felt a very weird feeling inside. I told him I could stay home, but he encouraged me to go. We talked about how we both wanted to go together in the rapture, and we prayed neither one of us had to live without the other. We both loved each other so deeply. It was a rather deep conversation, especially over fast food, but for some reason I just needed him to know I didn't want to live without him.

We enjoyed our time together with our friends at square dancing. That night I asked if I could dedicate and sing a song to Raymon. The leader and caller allowed me to do so.

I sang "You Light Up My Life" by Debby Boone. I wanted to share with everyone how much Raymon meant to me. He did indeed light up my life.

Raymon and I were best friends, and we weathered a lot of the storms together. When you are in the military away from everyone, you have to cling to each other. We were battle buddies. We were an "Army of one".

"The Dance"

Looking back on the memory of
The dance we shared 'neath the stars above
For a moment all the world was right
How could I have known that you'd ever say goodbye

And now I'm glad I didn't know
The way it all would end the way it all would go
Our lives are better left to chance I
could have missed the pain
But I'd have had to miss the dance

Tony Arata, composer

CHAPTER II

The Entrance Into My Tunnel

Raymon was leaned over and wrapped around me when I woke up on Wednesday morning. He was dressed in his uniform and ready to walk out the door. I was a bit surprised Raymon was lovingly laid over me the way he was, but it was very sweet. I believe he was praying for me to be safe going to Virginia later that day or possibly just wanting to say goodbye. We kissed, rubbed noses, and said "I love you." He went downstairs and out the door.

The first thing on my to-do list that day was to go to a board meeting for PWOC. I had something very special to tell them. I had a dream the night before that was really heavy on my heart, and I wanted to relay the message that was so vitally important.

The message was this: Do not be so overly invested in rituals and traditions with this group that you overlook the needs of the people. In my dream, I was the one who was having a huge problem and I was running to the staff of this church and asking them for help. They were putting me off because they had their agenda to contend with. I was frantically telling them I needed help and I needed it now. They just continued to push me to the side and proceeded with their scheduled agenda. I let my board know that in no uncertain terms did we ever have to fulfill our schedule to the point that we sacrificed ministering to a woman that attended our group. By the looks on their faces, they appeared to have received the message.

Melinda, the VP of our board, drove me to the airport after the meeting so I would not have to pay for airport parking. I left my car at Fort McPherson. All the way to the airport, I felt so anxious. I did not want to leave Raymon, my battle buddy, alone. My heart was beating so fast, and I was not feeling any peace whatsoever.

Melinda tried to comfort me and told me everything would be fine. I had not left Raymon's side since he was having the daytime episodes in November. Raymon had done so well the last month and encouraged me over and over that he would be just fine. He told me he had peace about me going.

I flew home, and as soon as I landed in Newport News I called Raymon. He sounded relieved that I made it. I was there to celebrate my dad's birthday. Living in Germany for the last three years, I had missed a lot of celebrations. Now that I was in the United States, my hope was to not miss one more family birthday.

Raymon could not come with me because he had to work. The Army had given him a good part of January to be home and get some rest because of all that he was going through. I really felt he was on the way to getting better and on his way to full recovery. I called Raymon several times to check on him and simply because I missed him a lot.

I came so close to canceling my trip because I was so nervous about leaving Raymon. When we had gotten home from square dancing Tuesday night, I got a call from my mom telling me that my sister was in the emergency room. Dawn's blood pressure was very high, and the nurse made a terrible mistake that nearly caused Dawn to lose her life. When I got off the phone, Raymon wrapped his loving arms around me and said, "See. You need to go home." That is the only reason I never changed my flight plans. My family would not have known any difference because I was making this a surprise visit. I wanted my Dad to be surprised for his birthday.

Now I was in Newport News, and my sister was home doing fine. In fact, we as a family went out to celebrate my Dad's birthday at my Dad's favorite restaurant and regular hangout. I put Raymon on the speaker phone so he could have a couple moments with us. Now that I had that special time with my family I wanted to be right back home with Raymon.

On Thursday, the day after I arrived in Newport News, Raymon told me he didn't sleep well the first night that I was away because I was not there. This only made me want to be home even more.

One of the many times I called Raymon on Thursday was because my sister Dawn and Jack, her fiancé, wanted to go see the movie *Astronaut Farmer*. This was a movie I really thought Raymon would want to see, so I wanted to check if it would be okay to see it with Dawn and Jack. Raymon let me know that it was fine with him and to have a good time. I so wished he was with me. The movie included a very sweet love story between a husband and his wife. This only made me long to be with Raymon. I called him as soon as we were out of the theater. He sounded energetic and in great spirits. This made me feel relieved that he was doing well.

Raymon called me before he went to sleep on Thursday night. I was surrounded by family with lots of talking and noise from the TV. We talked about the terrible tornado that hit Enterprise, Alabama that day. We were concerned about our friends we still had there. Because of all the noise around me, we cut our conversation short. As always, we said we loved each other, and I told him I would call him the next day. When I look back on our conversation, he sounded a bit weary of something, and I felt it was more than the tornado. He was my rock, and Raymon was not easily shaken.

I woke up the next morning around 7:30 a.m. to a call from our alarm company. The woman on the phone was a bit more frantic than our normal false-alarm call responders. She woke me up out of a deep sleep. She was asking me if I wanted her to send the police because multiple sensors were going off. I told her I needed to get off the phone and call my husband.

I wanted Raymon to tell me everything was OK. She strongly encouraged me to let her call the police. I said to go ahead.

I called Raymon's cell phone, and all I got was his voice mail. I called his office phone. The captain in his department answered. I asked to speak to Major George. The captain asked me where I was, and I told him I was in Virginia, even though I thought the whole department knew. He said, "Amy, can you hold a moment?" I said, "Sure," hoping he was going to give the phone to Raymon.

He came back on the phone and said, "Amy, I am so sorry, but Raymon has passed during his sleep sometime during the night." He informed me the whole department was on their way down to my house. They were a band of brothers. He asked me for my phone number, but my mind was totally frozen like a locked- up computer. I felt as if a pinball were going back and forth between my temples. I had to tell him I didn't know my number. He assured me he would get in touch with me.

Right before this call I had heard the Lord say to me, *Be still and know I am God.* After I got this horrific news, my soul would not cooperate. I screamed uncontrollably.

My mom, who is handicapped, got up from her bed to her wheelchair. I was in the step-down room adjacent to the living room, so she could only roll to the doorway of my room. She assumed I was having a nightmare and tried to wake me up. She loudly called out repeatedly, "Amy, Amy, wake up!" She did not know in that moment I was experiencing the worst nightmare of my life. I kept screaming. I had never before in my life come close to such traumatic pain and the uncontrollable responses I was having.

My mom called to my dad upstairs. It seemed like only a moment before he was by my side. He swooped me up in his strong arms and kept saying, "Hold on to Jesus. Hold on to Jesus." I had not felt his strong arms hold me like that since I was a little girl crying out in the night.

After my wordless screams of terror, I screamed, "I can't do this! I can't do this!"

My mom just looked at me with tears in her eyes, looking so helpless. My mom then called my sister. "Dawn, get here now." Thankfully, Dawn lived only five minutes away.

How ironic that what brought me home was the scare of possibly losing my sister and now it was my sister that was rushing to my side because my heart was shattered to pieces.

Next thing I knew, my older sister was there. It is amazing how everyone will react differently in a tragic moment. She tried to get me to lay my head in her lap. I did not want to lie down. I was inconsolable.

She took my phone and hit redial. She was the older sister. She demanded to know what was going on. Why was her baby sister screaming and crying in so much pain? I had told them Raymon was gone, but that was not enough information. She could not believe the tragic news. She had to hear it officially and with more of the details.

Soon, there was a detective on the other end of the call asking me questions. I just kept asking her if this was really happening. She said she was so sorry and it was really happening. She assured me they would take care of everything. I could not believe I was not there while all those police, medics, and friends filled my house, surrounding my Raymon.

The next thing I did was call my friend Becky. I immediately knew she had been notified of Raymon's departure when she answered the phone in a high pitch cry. She was the Chaplain's wife and the unit must have just notified him. There was extreme sadness and compassion in her voice. She had always been such a comforting and encouraging friend. On many occasions, I told her she reminded me of an angel. How I longed for an angel to soothe my pain.

Jack helped carry me to the bathroom. I had no strength in my body whatsoever. Dawn did what only big sisters will do and sat with me in the bathroom. I wasn't sure if it was for support or fear I would do something awful to myself.

A very sweet couple from my mom's church whom I have known for years arrived to see me. They sat on each side of me and both of them held each of my hands. I really believe no two better people could have been there at this moment. They were so tender and loving. I knew God had sent them to me. They left so I could rest.

My sister and Jack placed me on the couch in the living room to rest. I was so depleted. Shortly after I was on the couch, I had to run to the bathroom to vomit. I could hear my sister in the background saying she knew I would vomit from all of the grief. I suppose it is not just a movie thing.

My dearest friends came over. They hugged me and sat close. My mom sat over me like a protective mother hen. She didn't say anything but just lovingly sat close.

I couldn't eat anything. I tried once, and it didn't work well. In the evening, Dad offered to get me a milkshake. Even in my darkest night, ice cream always works. I knew my dad was having a very difficult time seeing his baby girl deal with my deep grief. I really believe it meant so much to him that he could offer me something that would be of comfort and get something in my stomach. I reached out and held his hand as I drank my milkshake.

My youth pastor, who was still a very good friend and mentor in my life, called and encouraged me saying, "Amy, it is okay to cry, to scream, and whatever reaction that comes as long and as loud as you need to." It gave me freedom to go at the pace I needed to go into my tunnel.

My best friend, Pam, who introduced me to my sweet husband, urged me to take a drive with her and get some fresh air. I did. It was the first time in my life that I can recall the sky being just a sky. I am someone who very much appreciates God's nature and creation. That day it was just a blue sky, and I felt no appreciation for it whatsoever.

I could not believe my Raymon was gone. He was my safe place on this earth. I could not believe I was abandoned. It is amazing how you can be surrounded by people and still feel so alone.

That night as I lay in bed to attempt to sleep, I heard the Lord say to my spirit, *My thoughts are not your thoughts and My ways are not your ways. My thoughts are higher than your thoughts. My ways are higher than your ways.* He said it with such authority and strength. I could not say anything in reply. I just understood that He is God and I am not.

The next day, I found myself comforting my mom with the very words God had spoken to my heart. She was very upset and even questioned her faith after interceding for Raymon's healing for so long. There are so many questions and thoughts when someone tragically and suddenly leaves us, yet God assured me He was in control.

I was scheduled to go home on Tuesday. The detective and Raymon's department informed me not to rush home because they had to take Raymon to the GBI (Georgia Bureau of Investigation) for an autopsy. This procedure was in vain since they did not come up with anything. His death certificate reads "Probable Seizure Disorder." This conclusion is due to the ongoing care he was receiving at the time.

I still wanted to get home, and I knew there was a lot to do to prepare for Raymon's funeral and memorials.

The earliest I could fly home was Sunday; two days after Raymon went home to Heaven. I was so anxious to get to Fayetteville, but God always knows best. I realized God was giving me an extra day to breathe before I was faced with the responsibility of so many decisions.

Karen, a dear friend of mine from Richmond, drove to Newport News to be with me on Saturday. She was my matron of honor at our wedding. The amazing thing about this is that we were out of touch for a very long time. She had no idea I was visiting Virginia and she called me on Thursday night. She said that God had put me strongly on her heart and she wanted to drive the ninety minute journey to visit me. I called her Friday to tell her the news. We both knew then why God had strongly put me on her heart on Thursday.

She drove me down to Fort Monroe, my favorite place to walk and meditate. This is also where Raymon proposed to me on February 14, 1999. She made a CD of some songs she thought would be encouraging to me. One of those songs was "Praise You In This Storm" by Casting Crowns. She held me close on the bench, the same bench on which I started my journey with Raymon. The song spoke the words of my heart.

Later that evening, we attempted to celebrate my dad's birthday. His party that was scheduled for Friday night was canceled due to Raymon going home to Heaven. Instead, we went to a local café with my immediate family and Karen. I had to excuse myself from the table a few times to go outside and just breathe. This fact remains: No matter if your life has just crumbled, life still goes on.

Karen stayed the night. Sometime during the night, I found myself cuddled next to Raymon. My arm was securely around him. It was so comforting and sweet. I suddenly realized I was holding Raymon. I then attempted quickly to turn him around to see his face. Shocked, I heard Karen's voice. My heart broke. It was a dream, or was it?

Later that morning, Karen drove my sister and me to the airport. Crazy enough, I had to be stopped in security to be searched. We headed home on my first flight as a widow. It was the first time in my entire life I could care less if the plane went down.

My sister and I took the long ride up the escalator to be greeted at Hartsfield-Jackson Atlanta International Airport by a lieutenant colonel in full uniform and his wife. My sister continued to say, "Just breathe. All I want you to do is concentrate on breathing." To this day, my heart still feels twinges of pain when I ride up this same escalator as I arrive home from my many travels.

When I first laid eyes on the uniformed lieutenant colonel who gave me my official notice, I could only think of Raymon dressed in the same uniform. Raymon always looked so handsome in his officer uniforms. This officer was Raymon's battle buddy over in Iraq. He tenderly smiled at me as if he knew what I was thinking. He gave me a moment to collect my thoughts. He then began his dutiful speech with, "On behalf of the president of the United States and the Army, we offer our condolences." I was given the military's official notice that every military spouse or family member hopes and prays they never have to hear. His wife and my friend, who was standing right behind him, stepped forward and handed me a beautiful bouquet of flowers. She presented them on behalf of all the army wives.

I was crying when Raymon's battle buddy offered his arm to begin escorting me down the hall. The USO representative assigned to greet soldiers tapped me on the back. He said, "Ma'am, please accept our sympathy." As we continued on our long solemn walk, suddenly a beautiful gesture of applause began from the large crowd who were awaiting their family and friends. It's the only time in my life where I felt such love and appreciation from a large group of strangers. Somehow in that moment we were not strangers but Americans unified by our loss.

Raymon's mother was coming in from Texas about the same time. I was escorted over to where her gate was. Security escorted her through to get to me. The moment I saw her, I broke down. We embraced tightly like never before. Our greatest pain merged into one. We were escorted into a room off to the side so we could continue our time together in privacy.

My sister was on luggage duty. She always feels better when she is taking care of the task at hand. We all met up at the military van out front of baggage claim. I was on my way home to a place where I had once shared an exciting new beginning with Raymon, where I would now begin my life as a widow.

Ladies from Protestant Women of the Chapel were waiting for me in the driveway. I got out of the van as they began to walk towards me. Seeing their sweet faces, I began to break down again. My chaplain and his wife had just arrived at the house. We had to call the police who let us in the back door using their masterful skills. Of all days, I could not find my key to open the house door. The police officer happened to be the same one who broke into our house to find Raymon in his bed.

Entering the house was one of the most painful things I had to face. My legs gave way and I crumbled. My chaplain took my hand and with his strong voice said, "Take your time." I thought it was a little odd when he said it, but I now know those were the most comforting words I needed to hear. "Take your time!"

My chaplain and my friend Nancy helped me up, and sat close to me on my lounge chair. They were giving me what I needed desperately— the comfort of their presence.

I was ready to survey my new home. I wanted to go alone, but Nancy took my hand and accompanied me. Everything seemed so different even though it was the same. The hardest room to go into was Raymon's room. He continued to have his own room even though we slept together more often. I laid my chest on the bed where he last breathed. I so longed to be close to him.

*Raymon and I at our last Christmas Ball
(Picture used for his Army memorial)*

Chapter III

Glorify And Honor

I so appreciated my friends and family around me. They came from Virginia, Texas, Indiana, Washington, D.C., and Kentucky, all to our house we had just purchased six months previously. Ironically, one of the things we had loved about the house was how open and hospitable it was. I never would have imagined I would be hosting the first fifty-plus people in it without Raymon. Most of these guests were on his side of the family. I would have loved to have seen his smile seeing all of his family gathered together here in his home.

We had four different occasions to memorialize my sweet husband. My prayer was that they would all bring glory to Jesus and be honorable to my husband. God answered this prayer at each ceremony.

The first ceremony was Raymon's army memorial. The family and I were placed in a small room to gather with the generals and the chaplain. General Russel Honoré was the four-star general who commanded First Army, my husband's division. He was also the general who oversaw the military relief efforts for

Hurricane Katrina. This man had walked alongside presidents.

General Honoré visited my home on Monday afternoon, the day after I came home from Virginia, with his staff. He was so gentle and kind. He encouraged me, "Amy, you will not ever get over this, but you will get through it because of your great faith." I was not aware he had known me in this personal way.

And now, he placed his arm around me as we circled to pray. The chaplain prayed a beautiful prayer, and then we formed a line to walk out and join the other soldiers. They began to play the song that I had requested, "God Bless the USA" by Lee Greenwood.

This song meant a lot to Raymon. Every time Raymon and I would hear it at different functions, I would see tears in his eyes. He loved his country very much. The last time I had sung this song I was celebrating his homecoming from the war, and now this very beautiful patriotic song was being played to honor Raymon and his homegoing to Heaven. His final war was now forever over.

When we walked out to take our seats, I saw one of the most beautiful sights I had ever seen. There had to be over two hundred soldiers in uniform standing at attention. Directly in front of me, I saw military boots, an aviator helmet, and Raymon's dog tags displayed next to our formal picture we had taken at our last Christmas Ball. A female soldier I had met at a unit picnic when we first moved to Atlanta began to sing our National Anthem. The heaviness of the moment made her struggle to continue, so I joined in singing with her. The others joined in as well. It was a unified moment as one big military family.

The ceremony was touching for so many reasons. The men in his department led the memorial. I so appreciated how Raymon's battle buddy had collected e-mails from some dear friends and fellow soldiers Raymon had worked with over the past several years. I was so surprised. The words they were saying about Raymon made me smile.

They honored Raymon with the twenty-one gun salute and "Taps." They also had a ceremony called the Roll Call. This is a ceremony where a drill sergeant calls out several different soldiers' names and they respond with an affirmative answer. The sergeant then called out, "Major Raymon George!" Silence followed. Again he yelled, "Major Raymon Edward George!" Again, silence. Again he yelled louder, "Major Raymon George!" Nothing but silence. This moment was so powerful. The silence echoed so loudly, "Your husband is no longer here."

The chaplain did a beautiful job on the message. Raymon would have been so pleased. This was the same chaplain who had offered Raymon encouragement and support since our arrival in Georgia. His wife, Becky, was also a dear friend to me. We had met at a retreat I was in charge of when we were stationed in Alabama. The spring retreat was wonderful, but I unexpectedly lost my Granny Hendley to Heaven the morning I left for the retreat. I could not cancel because I was in charge of it all. During our down time at the retreat, Becky helped me prepare the song I sang at my granny's funeral, "Victory in Jesus." Now Becky was my angel again playing the piano before and after my husband's memorial. She encouraged me with her sweet, reassuring smile that said, "I am here."

As I stood at the door shaking hands and receiving hugs from all of my military family, the coworker who kindly gave Raymon daily rides to work introduced himself. He was the one who called the police that dreadful morning when he noticed Raymon was not waiting outside for him. Raymon was very thoughtful and punctual. He also appreciated his coworker's generosity. Meeting Raymon's coworker was one of many touching moments in the receiving line.

The family and I went home and rested until the viewing that night. Our families sat around and talked about Raymon all day. I was so grateful to have everyone with me. The families were getting to know each other like never before. This was one of the sun rays that shined through my dark clouds during this time.

I left early for the funeral home to take his dad, who had arrived from Florida, to see Raymon for the first time. When we arrived, the Patriot Guard was standing outside with their flags.

They are a wonderful group of veterans and volunteers who care deeply about soldiers and their families. They ride their motorcycles and stand guard against any distractions to the deceased soldier's family at the memorial services that honor the soldiers.

I said hello and ushered his dad inside. I was prepared for the worst. I could not even feel my legs the first time I had visited Raymon the day before. When I saw Raymon lying there in the casket, I knew he was indeed gone. He had been so full of life even with all the difficulties he faced. Now, his spirit was absent. He looked so old. His body reflected the hardship and the exhaustion he endured for the last three and a half years.

I walked into the viewing room on his dad's arm. I could not believe what happened next. There was a wave of peace and joy that washed over me. I knew instantly it was God's grace carrying me through the evening.

I visited with Raymon, and then I greeted the Patriot Guard outside. They were so gentle and kind despite their rough motorcyclist appearance. I went back in the viewing room to stand by Raymon and wait for family and friends.

I stood by Raymon all night long, because I wasn't about to leave his side now. All the family and friends stood in line and greeted us one by one. I stood there with a smile on my face and hugged each one, offering an encouraging word. "Raymon is no longer suffering. He is with the Lord." I could not have done this if it wasn't for the amazing grace of God.

I have heard and sung about the joy of the Lord, but it wasn't until that very moment I truly knew what it was. Regardless of our circumstances, the joy of the Lord is our strength.

AMY BIRCHFIELD

Do not grieve, for the joy of the LORD is your strength.

Nehemiah 8:10b (NIV)

After everyone paid their respects, they watched the video of Raymon's life put together with music he absolutely loved. These were songs like "Splish Splash" and "Old Time Rock and Roll". I also included songs that were special to us, like "The Power of Love", our first dance at our wedding, "My Special Angel" and "You Light Up My Life". It was a beautiful tribute to honor Raymon's life. My mom sat across the room the whole time, keeping a watchful eye on me. My mom truly has the most comforting and sweet smile.

My Mom's smile has always been the "Wind Beneath My Wings".

My mom and dad were the last ones to leave the room, but before my dad walked out he looked at me with Daddy's loving eyes and gave me the sweetest hug. I know he must have never thought he would see his baby girl have to stand beside her husband's casket.

When I was alone in the room, I began to look at all of the beautiful flowers and read all the beautiful notes from those who had sent them. I had time to talk to Raymon alone.

"Raymon, I am very proud of you. You died for the country you loved, and you are my hero too." He had told me when we were dating that he wanted to give me the world. He did just that and more. I told him, "I love you, and I always will."

The next day was Raymon's funeral. It was nice to have a memorial to honor him as a soldier, but today's service was to honor him for being Raymon. It was a beautiful sunny day, and our family and friends met at the funeral home. One of the highlights of this day was seeing people I had not seen in such a long time. A very special couple Raymon and I knew in Alabama was waiting for me when I arrived. This couple had been such a great support to us in our first years of marriage. They were our best friends in Alabama. I had not seen them since our goodbyes when we were leaving for Germany. I could not believe they would not ever see Raymon again. It was time for Raymon's tribute to begin. The staff at the funeral home escorted everyone out to their cars.

The staff gave his parents and me some alone time with Raymon before the processional to the chapel. When we walked out to go to our car, it was so touching to see everyone stand beside their car to pay their respects. The staff rolled Raymon's casket out behind us and placed him in the hearse. I was asked by one of the Patriot Guard if I wanted to ride on his motorcycle. I so wish I had not turned him down.

Our motorcade drove over twenty miles to arrive at Fort McPherson. We arrived one hour before the funeral to give others time to pay their respects. The altar in Fort McPherson's chapel, the chapel where we attended Sunday services, was the last place where I saw Raymon's face. Right beside him inside the casket lay a heart of flowers. It consisted of seven red roses for each year we were married and one white rose, which symbolized the hope of eternity where we would be together forever. I placed my hand on his chest one last time and said my final goodbye. The funeral home staff escorted all the family out so we would not see the closing of his casket.

I went through the doorway they led us into, and I made my way right back around so I was standing at the back of the chapel. I wanted to be there to the very end. I had a sweet chaplain who had endured the loss of his wife to cancer a few years earlier. He placed his arm around my shoulder as we watched together. I knew he knew the pain.

For I Know The Plans

    The family and I came down the aisle to our seats to the song "Rockin' Robin" by Bobby Day. Yes, I said "Rockin' Robin." This was Raymon's style of music. He told me on numerous occasions that if his funeral was sad and daunting, he would be so mad. I never imagined that I would have to fulfill this wish so early into our marriage. So Raymon, I know you will be pleased with me and say "Thank you" when I see you again.

    We then began the service with two of his favorite praise songs, "Days of Elijah" by Robin Mark and "Shout to the Lord" by Darlene Zschech. All of the chaplains had a part in the service. Instead of one person sharing the eulogy, I gave the opportunity to anyone who wanted to share their memories of Raymon. Our plan was for his mom to open this special time and for me to close it.

    Many people, from various parts of Raymon's life, came up to speak. It was a beautiful display of what a wonderful person Raymon truly was. One person alone could not have done Raymon justice. I really believe it also did a lot of good for those who were hurting. They wanted to express their love and appreciation for Raymon to those who were there. We cried and laughed. It was so beautiful. I hugged each person when they came down from speaking.

    The service had so many special moments. The female soldier who had sung the National Anthem the day before came up and shared something that happened at work. She said that she was wearing a slogan shirt that said "Got Jesus?" and Raymon said to her in passing, "Yes. I do." She wasn't sure at first what he meant, and then he pointed at her shirt. She was so happy to know at that moment he was also a believer in Jesus Christ. She was sharing how such a passing moment at work meant a lot to her knowing Raymon was in Heaven.

Another special moment was when his commander from Germany came up to speak. He was talking about Raymon's character and how he had learned so much from Raymon even though he was Raymon's leader. He was so impressed with Raymon and how he was such an unassuming guy. He did everything with excellence. This commander and his wife drove four hours from Alabama to be at Raymon's funeral.

When it was time for me to speak, I could not wait to tell everyone what a special husband Raymon was to me. I was told later by my sister, "You patted Raymon's casket several times through your talk. It was so sweet." I was unaware I did this but glad they could see the love I had for him.

I started from the beginning. We met on my twenty-sixth birthday. Our first date started at a restaurant that had closed too early, and Raymon had to make other arrangements. He had called our friend Pam, our matchmaker, to arrange to go to her house. We played cards with Pam and her husband. This actually made things more comfortable for us, especially with us just meeting. Raymon looked across the table at me with adoration in his eyes while we played Spades as partners. No one had ever looked at me like that before. We won that night. It was the beginning of our wonderful journey together. He truly was the best birthday present I have ever received from the Lord.

I shared how we attended a memorial ceremony together the Thursday before our wedding. He was out on the field saluting while I stood directly in front of him in the stands with my hand over my heart while a bugler played "Taps". It was truly sobering how I knew even then that this day could come because of his life as a soldier.

Raymon was my hero. He met and married me when I was such a broken woman, and God used him in my life to bring a deep healing to my heart. He knew how to love me. He separated those things I did from the hurtful place in my heart and treated me like the lady he knew I truly was. He would say things like, "Amy, I know that is your hurt talking." It truly is a blessing when someone can love you in this way.

I shared a little song we would always sing to each other as a display of our love. It goes like this:

You're my lover. You're my friend.
You're my beginning and my end.
Your love is all around me,
When the world just walks away.
You're the sunshine on a cloudy day.
You're the one who washes my blues away.
You can always count on me.
You're my lover. You're my friend.

Raymon would always give the last note a nice southern drawl *"fri-end."*

The most important thing I shared that day was that Raymon is with the Lord. He wanted nothing more than for every single person to be with him in Heaven one day. I encouraged everyone to make sure things were right between them and the Lord.

I declared at the end of my speech that I would share our story for the rest of my life. Writing this book is a big part of fulfilling this declaration. I finished by telling Raymon, "Thank you for the gift of you. I love you."

When I sat down, the song Raymon had always dedicated to me since our wedding day, "My Special Angel" began to play. Raymon always called me his Special Angel. The truth be told, I felt he was my special angel, especially now.

The last chaplain came up and did an amazing job giving a beautiful, powerful word about Raymon and Heaven. He ended by singing "I Can Only Imagine" by Mercy Me. Everyone later told me it was truly the best funeral they had ever attended.

The song "Untitled Hymn" by Chris Rice began. This was the cue for our exit. I was escorted out by CJ, the owner and director of the funeral home.

CJ was the one who came to our home and pronounced Raymon deceased. When planning the funeral, he knelt beside me and explained everything he saw that morning. This was something I wanted to know, and it meant a lot to me that he took the time to walk me through what he saw and experienced. It was a blessing to hear that he felt Raymon was prepared to go. He said, "He might not have been ready, but I could tell he was prepared to go to Heaven." He also said something so true. "Heaven just got even sweeter for you, Amy."

When he escorted me out, I released a dove into the sky. When I did, the dove flew up and made a full circle around the flag-pole and then flew over our heads. It was so touching to experience this. It was an act of surrendering Raymon to the Lord.

I stood at the bottom of the steps greeting everyone and receiving sympathies.

Raymon was then escorted out and placed into the hearse. I stood there looking at his flag-draped casket. It would be the last time I saw him until he arrived at his final resting place in Arlington National Cemetery.

After everyone went home to their respective homes, it was a very empty house. It had been a whirlwind of events and people, and now I was faced with a lonely house. What was next? I just sat there feeling the hollowness of it all. I knew that if I screamed, I would only hear my echo yelling back. I felt not only the absence of my husband but also somehow the absence of God in a way that was very scary. The reality of my life became very cold.

Let me encourage you who know what this feels like: God is there. The enemy of your soul would love to discourage and bully you into thinking He is not, but I assure you God is there. He is so close!

> **The LORD is close to the brokenhearted; he rescues those whose spirits are crushed.**
>
> *Psalm 34:18(NLT)*

He gently let me know in so many different ways that He was close. He sent me a beautiful sign to show me shortly after everyone went home. I was sitting on my loveseat, and I was very concerned about the next step in my life. I felt lost and stripped of everything I highly valued. What was I going to do? What would happen to me now? Suddenly, I looked down on the arm of the loveseat, and there was a little slip of paper from my box of Bible references. It said Ruth 3:11. I did not know what this particular verse was so I hurried to find my Bible.

It stated:

> **And now, my daughter, fear not; I will do to thee all that thou requirest: for all the city of my people doth know that thou art a virtuous woman.**
>
> *Ruth 3:11 (KJV)*

I truly felt the Father's love in this moment. I know He will share His love with you in a very personal way.

Finally, it was time to lay Raymon to rest in Arlington National Cemetery. His funeral was held on March 10, 2007. We had to wait till March 29 to lay him to rest because of the waiting list of soldiers to be laid to rest there.

I was escorted by Raymon's boss and his battle buddy to Washington, D.C. on March 28. Raymon would have been proud of how these two men cared for me that day. I was the only one from the Atlanta area who would be attending the Arlington service. His family and friends would all meet us either at the hotel or at the cemetery. His mom and sister were at the hotel when I arrived.

My friend Karen drove up from Richmond to be by my side just as she was at our wedding. We went to dinner with an old family friend who lived in the D.C. area. After dinner, he walked us up the steps of the Capitol building. It was such a beautiful night. I was able to look across the mall area up to the Washington Monument. It was so peaceful. We then walked around the Capitol to the Supreme Court Building. My friend felt led to pray for me there. It was very appropriate. Many major decisions were made in that building that affect us today, and now I was dealing with many major decisions of my own.

We went back to our hotel to get ready for the next day. My mom and sister drove up from Newport News with my nephew, Jonathan. Raymon and I had the privilege of having Jonathan live with us in his junior and senior years of high school. He was now twenty-three years old. Raymon and Jonathan had formed a wonderful bond while he lived with us.

I spent some time with my mom in her room before I called it a night. Everyone else went downstairs. I felt like a scared little girl longing for the comfort and security of her mother's love. She just held me.

I was so thankful Karen was sharing the room with me because the last thing I wanted was to be left alone.

The next morning came early. We all met downstairs at the breakfast buffet. Jonathan was wondering why I was not more upset. He let me know it was OK to allow myself to feel the overwhelming sadness of this day. I told him I simply had the peace of God with me.

The limousine arrived to drive Raymon's mom, sister, Karen, and me to Arlington. The others were driving in their own cars. We all lined up at the entrance of the gate waiting for permission to enter.

While sitting there, a couple of us noticed we had friends lined up in their cars behind us. We got out of the car and I said hello to friends from Germany. I also saw a dear couple who was in our wedding. I had not seen them since that day because of the military moves we all had made. We got back into the limousine.

Next we rode to the Welcome Center where we all met to prepare for the graveside ceremony. Riding through this cemetery for the first time was such a solemn time, the final ride to face the reality of letting go of Raymon.

To see the headstones of all the soldiers that had gone before and knowing my husband was about to join them was so heart wrenching, but also I knew what an honor to lay Raymon beside these very honorable men and women was a way I could pay tribute to Raymon.

I was happy to see the women from PWOC (Protestant Women of the Chapel) in that area whom I was not expecting. Their support meant a lot to me.

The general from Fort Gillem in Atlanta had me and Raymon's mom and dad sit on a couch. This is when he presented each of us with a flag case. I was not expecting to see such a beautiful wooden case and what was inside. When I opened it, it had Raymon's military ribbons arranged the way he wore them on his chest. It was very moving to see them. We also received our Gold Star pins. When we grow up we try to achieve the gold stars for recognition or accomplishment, but this was one gold star I definitely did not want to obtain. Raymon deserved the gold star for his life on this earth, but as I told him many times I know God had a wonderful crown awaiting him for putting up with me.

We were escorted from the meeting room to our cars. This is when I saw Raymon's casket in the back of the hearse. The limousine followed behind the hearse until we made a stop about a hundred feet ahead. We got out of the cars to watch Raymon's casket be transferred from the hearse to the horse-drawn carriage. What I had not expected was a full band in uniform playing the most beautiful music such as "Faith of Our Fathers". While watching this beautiful, honorable ceremony, I was shaking from head to toe. This was the first time I felt the extreme finality and reality of the moment.

My sister later told me she had an eye on me in case I fainted. I got back into the limousine to follow behind the horse carriage carrying my sweet Raymon and the army of soldiers marching behind it. I was about to break down. Suddenly I could hear Raymon, in my soul, tell me a funny story I will always remember.

He reminded me of a parade I attended. At that time, Raymon was a captain and company commander at Fort Eustis, Virginia. In the parade, Raymon led his company in formation when the announcer called him Captain Ramon Jorge instead of Raymon George.

It was the funniest thing, because my husband had no Hispanic blood in him. When I heard Raymon remind me of this story, I kept my head down and smiled. It was the perfect time and was exactly what I needed. It broke the extreme grief that was overwhelming me.

All through the very somber march to his final resting place, I heard Raymon tell me, *It is not me, Amy, it is only my body.* He also told me he was thankful he didn't have to march in those army-issued shoes. When we got to his final resting place, we were escorted out of our cars. We were asked to stand in front of our chairs on the first row. The soldiers honorably raised the flag above Raymon's casket. We stood there in silence. It was a blessing to be in this special place in peace and quiet. It was a moment where I could catch my breath and pause in this rapidly moving ceremony of letting Raymon go.

In the distance, we heard the sound of helicopters. The five helicopters were getting louder and louder until they flew over us, paying respect to their fallen fellow aviator. I was so thankful the Army honored Raymon with this fly by. Raymon loved being a helicopter pilot.

What I felt was so ironic was that Raymon flew in this very airspace with many VIP missions to the Pentagon, which sat right behind where we were standing. I wondered whether Raymon had a feeling he would lie right here one day. This I will not ever know until I see him again in Heaven.

The service continued with Arlington's chaplain saying a few words. My prayer was answered again. God was glorified and Raymon was honored. I was amazed how a man that never knew Raymon could do such an incredible job of getting it right. I had spoken to him on the phone when I was back in Atlanta. He was so kind and attentive. He asked me a lot of wonderful questions about Raymon to prepare for this day. After that conversation, I came to realize something very special I wanted to add. I informed him at the Welcome Center.

Raymon had been encouraged the last couple of years reading his Daily Bread devotions. He always placed a check mark by the date to show he had read it. When I received his items from his workplace, I saw the devotional in his belongings. I could not wait to open it up and see if there was a check mark on the last day of his life, March 1. It was indeed marked. I was so blessed to know he had read God's word. The verse for that day sent chills down my spine.

> **Therefore, if anyone is in Christ, the new creation has come: The old has gone, the new is here!**
>
> *II Corinthians 5:17(NIV)*

Raymon was encouraged with these words on the last day of his life. The chaplain included this in his message, and he did so beautifully. After he spoke, the flag was folded and presented to me. His battle buddy did the honors. He spoke of how there are only two on this earth who will give their lives for me: the Lord Jesus Christ and a soldier. Raymon had so many qualities of Jesus in his character.

The twenty-one-gun salute was given followed by "Taps." I held the flag so close to my chest. Raymon's mom held me tight and whispered, "Remember, it is just his body." Yes, it was his body, but those arms were the ones that held me tight. Those lips were the ones I kissed goodnight. Those feet were the ones that danced with me and walked in to see me from work. I was so angry his body had failed him. His body could not keep up with his beautiful heart and spirit, and now I would have to live without seeing his beautiful smile until we meet again.

After the ceremony was over, his mom respectfully hurried me away from Raymon's casket. It wasn't until later I realized why she did that. They felt if I lingered I would never want to leave. I was not able to have that one last moment with him, but I encouraged myself by remembering that my last moment truly with him was the morning he embraced me before I left for Virginia.

All of the army officials presented me with a token of appreciation from high-ranking officials. I then was greeted by all those who attended in uniform, and several of those individuals were very dear friends and family members. I gave my mom a kiss and said goodbye to her and the rest of the guests who needed to return home.

Several of Raymon's family joined the original group of us in the limousine back to their house. Raymon's aunt and uncle hosted a luncheon. It was nice they lived in the area. I was also able to visit with my dear friends I had not seen since wedding day. After lunch, they drove Karen and me back to the hotel. I said my goodbyes to Karen, and I stayed a couple of more days in D.C. alone.

As I sat in my hotel room and thought back over the last month, I thanked the Lord for answering my prayers. God was glorified, and Raymon had indeed been honored in all of the memorials and funerals.

Visiting Raymon for our 8 year Anniversary in Arlington National Cemetery

CHAPTER IV

Depending On God

The next couple of days were very dark as I continued to stay alone in my hotel room. I felt the enemy more in those two days than ever before. I want to warn you that the enemy can play havoc with your mind when you are dealing with such a great loss. I had the worst fight on my hands. I pleaded my case before the Lord. I didn't understand why I had to fight this fight on top of grieving the loss of my husband. I felt in my spirit that Daddy God wanted me to trust Him. He wanted to teach me a few things about spiritual warfare. I was so scared, and I held on to Daddy God more in those dark hours than ever before. I was in the foxhole of life, and this felt like the ultimate war for survival.

I was lying prostrate on the floor praying and had the Christian radio station on in my hotel room. Suddenly, I felt absolutely frozen from the top of my head to the bottom of my feet. The first note of the song "More" by Matthew West began. One ear was pinned to the floor while the other was listening intently to the message.

I encourage you to listen to the song. It is the Father's heart towards us. I knew Daddy God was speaking a very clear message to me. HE LOVED ME!!! When the last note finished, the Lord released me from this frozen state. He wanted my undivided attention and He got it! He then spoke to my spirit. He informed me that I was about to experience a smidgen of His power. I felt this tremendous weight on me. It felt like tons of enormous weight. He said, *Amy, that is just an ounce of my power.*

When I got off the floor, my muscles were so fatigued and shaking. Daddy God began to speak to my spirit reminding me of His word:

> **What, then, shall we say in response to these things? If God is for us, who can be against us?**
>
> *Romans 8:31(NIV)*

God spoke in my spirit, *Amy, you do not have to fear what the enemy will try to do to you.* The Lord comforted me with this assurance. He was there!

I wanted to go to sleep so badly after this powerful time. The Lord tenderly encouraged me not to sleep but to go downstairs and get something to eat. I had no idea how I was going to get downstairs and fix a plate at the buffet feeling like this. When I did get down to the restaurant, the waitress was so kind and had me sit down. She fixed me a plate and waited on me. I really felt she was my angel that day.

I went back to my room and rested until the next round. The enemy was relentless. I wish I could say that after the wonderful, awesome encounter with God it was all over, but it was not.

God knew I needed my special time with Him to hold on to. The enemy wanted me to give in and take my life. I had a major suicidal spirit trying to take me out. The enemy knew if there was any chance of stealing my life, this was it.

He knew that when I got stronger, it was all over for him. I want you to know there is an enemy. He wants you dead. Do not give in!!! He knows the secret, and this is it. When you get stronger, and you will if you don't give up, you will have a powerful tool to use against him. It is called your overcoming testimony. It will destroy his plans.

There are two songs named "Victory" and "I Want It Back" both sung by Tye Tribbett that explains this very truth. Not only will *you* live a victorious life, but you will have a testimony to use as a weapon of destruction against satan for others. You will be the one to steal from satan what belongs to God. When you bring hope to others you will be doing just that.

You will be able to tell of the hope I am sharing with you now. Do not let the enemy win this fight. You hold on to Jesus' hand and do not let go. I am here to tell you the light is coming!

During my time in the hotel room, God was speaking to me about the hope He had for me to share. The verses found in Isaiah 61 were resounding strongly in my spirit. I opened the hotel Bible to this passage and it was as if the words were popping up off the page. God was affirming me with words of hope that my hell was not in vain. He had a plan and purpose and this is what He was declaring over me:

> **1The Spirit of the Lord GOD is upon me, Because the LORD has anointed me to bring good news to the afflicted; He has sent me to bind up the brokenhearted, to proclaim liberty to captives and freedom to prisoners;**
> **2To proclaim the favorable year of the LORD and the day of vengeance of our God; to comfort all who mourn,**
> **3To grant those who mourn in Zion, giving them a garland instead of ashes, the oil of gladness instead of mourning, the mantle of praise instead of a spirit of fainting. So they will be called oaks of righteousness, the planting of the LORD, that He may be glorified.**
>
> *Isaiah 61:1-3 (NASB)*

The one thing that is necessary through our tunnel of grief and loss is our dependence on God. Our relationship with God is vital for us to successfully make it through. God is close to us. Our responsibility in this relationship is to lay our head on His chest and depend on our Loving Father.

> This is the most important truth
> I could share with you:
> **Jesus Loves You**

³⁸ For I am convinced that neither death nor life, neither angels nor demons, neither the present nor the future, nor any powers, ³⁹ neither height nor depth, nor anything else in all creation, will be able to separate us from the love of God that is in Christ Jesus our Lord.

Romans 8:38-39 (NIV)

The morning I lost Raymon to Heaven I screamed, "I can't do this. I can't do this." God knew I could not face the loss of my husband on my own. You see, it wasn't until I did what He told me, *Be still and know I am God,* that I had any sense of peace. He never intended for us to walk the journey on our own. He knows the only way we are going to make this journey successfully is depending on Him.

> **For your Creator will be your husband; the LORD of Heaven's Armies is his name! He is your Redeemer, the Holy One of Israel, the God of all the earth. ⁶ For the**

> **LORD has called you back from your grief— as though you were a young wife abandoned by her husband,"** says your God. **⁷ "For a brief moment I abandoned you, but with great compassion I will take you back. ⁸ In a burst of anger I turned my face away for a little while. But with everlasting love I will have compassion on you,"** says the LORD, your Redeemer
>
> *Isaiah 54:5-8 (NLT)*

Just as with a marriage, it takes two in the relationship to make it work successfully. I can tell you I reminded the Lord on so many occasions of His promise. I reminded Him in simple as well as difficult things. For example, I called on Him when I had squirrels in my attic. I would say, "God, you are my husband, and I need those squirrels to stop making noise so I can sleep." Next thing I knew, He made them stop. Then He helped me find someone who helped me get them out for good. When I felt scared and alone, I would say aloud, "God, I know You are here with me, and I do not need to be afraid. You are my protector."

God has taught me through His word and experiences about the power of agreement. The power of agreement is a very important spiritual truth. This truth alone has helped me tremendously through the journey in my tunnel.

> **The tongue has the power of life and death, and those who love to talk will have to eat their own words.**
>
> *Proverbs 18:21(GWT)*

God's Word is true. We need to break agreement with the lie of the enemy and come into agreement with what God says about our situation. For example, there are times when fear tries to come and attack me. I have a choice right then to allow it to wreak havoc on my mind or break agreement with it. I simply declare, "I break agreement with this fear in the name of Jesus." I declare aloud, "I come into agreement with God's word that states:

> **For God did not give us a spirit of timidity (of cowardice, of craven and cringing and fawning fear), but [He has given us a spirit] of power and of love and of calm and well-balanced mind and discipline and self-control.**
>
> *2 Timothy 1:7 (AMP)*

God's Word is powerful!!! God has given us the choice to come into agreement with it or not. I choose to walk in freedom. I hope you will too.

AMY BIRCHFIELD

Handling Pain God's Way

The first night I was home as a widow, I set my alarm clock because there were many details to be decided the next morning. I heard in my spirit to set the CD on my alarm clock to number five. I had no idea what number five was on my CD, and I was too tired and weary to care. I just knew I would wake up to the song that was listed number five on the CD.

God has given us the beautiful retreat of sleep, but when I woke up I felt as if a Mack Truck were hitting me with a full dose of reality. I was in excruciating pain. My friend ran upstairs when she heard me wail and tried to console me, but the storm cloud did not pass for over an hour.

In my bedroom, I have a big window overlooking the backyard. It faces east, so the sun on most days would shine right on me. Every morning, I opened the window's blinds and raised my arms to Daddy God to say, "Good morning." I would thank Him for the new day and pray He would order my steps. I loved starting my day with Him. The sun shone brightly on me, and I would feel the warmth of His love. It gave me such joy.

This particular morning after the storm clouds rolled by, I looked at my window and I heard the Lord question me, *Are you coming to greet me this morning*? I was stunned at His question. To be honest, I thought surely He would give me a pass on this of all mornings. He was so patient with me as I looked down at the bed and up to the window and down again at my bed and up to the window. I am not exaggerating when I tell you it took me about an hour to think over this proposal. I gently and lovingly heard Him say to me, *Come to Me those who are weary and heavy laden and I will give you rest.* You see, I knew I had a choice. Am I going to handle this pain and grief on my own, or am I going to depend on my loving Father and do it His way?

I wish I could tell you I just sprang up and opened my blinds, but it took everything I had to get up and make the sacrifice of praise. The very second I lifted my arms, I felt the Lord consume my sacrifice and embrace me in a way I had never felt.

Also, in that very second my alarm clock came on with the song "I Can Only Imagine". I continued to worship the Lord for several minutes. One of the songs that followed "I Can Only Imagine" was "In Christ Alone" by Michael English. It was such an amazing and beautiful time with my Daddy God. Getting out of that bed was the best choice I ever made. I know without a shadow of a doubt it is the very reason I am here today.

Facing My Pain on My Own

I can also recall a time when I did not go to God for my pain and grief. It was another very dark time for me. My Granny Pierce and I were very close. This closeness was strengthened when I took on the responsibility of looking after her right after Grandad died. I was only eight years old. I hated the fact she was all alone, and I had a heart full of compassion for her. My granny recognized I wanted to be with her and help her. She appreciated it very much. She would always say, "I don't know what I would do without you." I would overhear her telling other people what a big help I was to her. My middle name, Lois, was her middle name and the name she went by. I loved being named after her. My dad told me one time that my looks did remind him of Granny, his mother. My granny and I had such a loving bond, and I loved her very much. Thankfully, she lived in close proximity to my family.

Granny Pierce, my first best friend

We would start our day by waking up in the two twin beds in her bedroom. We would have breakfast and get ready for the day, and then we went outside and sat on the bench swing where we planned our adventure for the day.

My granny did not have a driver's license, so we would take long walks to the store. We enjoyed taking walks through the woods and down the creek behind her house.

One year, we cut down a tree in her yard to use as a Christmas tree. It got a lot bigger when we brought it into the house. We would also rake leaves and burn them. Many a night we would sit at the dinner table and I would listen to all the stories of her upbringing and the Great Depression. I loved hearing her play her organ. My favorite song she would play that would fill the house was "How Great Thou Art" by Stuart K. Hine.

Granny Pierce's House
Drawn by John Pierce, my uncle.

I simply loved being with her. Her home gave me such comfort and peace. She was my safe place growing up. My parents worked a lot, and she was always the constant in my life.

When I was twenty years old, things started taking a turn for the worse. My granny was diagnosed with Alzheimer's disease. I lived with her the last year of her life. I gave her insulin shots for her diabetes and simply did damage control for a woman who still wanted to keep on moving. I will never forget the day I took a quick trip to the store for some groceries. I came back and she didn't remember who I was. This experience felt like a knife stab in my heart. Alzheimer's is a very sad and frustrating disease. I completely lost Granny Pierce to Heaven on August 6, 1993 when I was twenty-one years old.

I didn't turn to God for my source of comfort and strength. I turned to drinking and hanging out at the club dancing every night. I didn't want to feel the pain because it hurt so badly. I continued to live in her house without her. My family gave me this gift of staying just a little while longer to help with the pain of letting go. The house did get colder and colder without her. I came to realize the person is what makes the home. My family sold her home shortly after I moved in with a friend three months after her passing.

I continued to drink and hang out with other people who were hurting. The club is where a lot of people wear masks to avoid others seeing their pain. In fact, one of the women I hung out with was a widow. She was drowning her loss in smoking, dancing, and befriending people much younger than herself. She was running away from the pain just as much as I was.

My dismal routine went something like this: I worked a full-time job, I came home and took a nap, woke up, got ready, and went to the club. I would dance all night until the place closed at 2 a.m. Afterwards, I would join my friends at Denny's and stay there anywhere from an hour to sometimes four hours. I do not know how in the world I did that for a year.

I was running from the pain. Finally, the noise stopped. I was sitting at the club on a bar stool, and I heard Daddy God's voice in my spirit say, *It is time to go home.* I knew this time it was for good. I had been acting like a child who was pouting and closed off in her bedroom. I was mad at my Daddy God. He said, *Enough!*

Do you know what I got out of handling my pain on my own? I received absolutely nothing.

Did I honor my granny? No.

Did I make several bad choices along the way in all of that madness? Yes.

You know what I found at the end of that road? I found nothing but darkness and hollowness.

NOT LETTING GO

I lay down with Raymon in his bed one night several months before he passed. I was so happy to be there next to him, and he was snuggled up behind me with his arm tenderly embracing me. I felt so much love and comfort. The next moment was absolutely terrifying. He went into one of his PTSD episodes. He grabbed my arm so tightly that I could not release his fingers. When I did, he came back and scratched me so hard trying to grab on again. He eventually woke up from his episode and turned to go to the bathroom. He had no idea what had just happened. I, on the other hand, was devastated.

I went to my bathroom down the hall and just cried. My arm was throbbing. I went from feeling so loved and comforted to being in a nightmare. I thought about how I had dealt with my pain on my own. I knew it had led to a dead end. I told the Lord that night, "No matter what, I am not letting go of You."

This is a decision only you can make. Are you going to handle your pain and grief your way, which will lead only to greater darkness? Or are you going to give it to your Loving Father? When you give God your pain, you will be comforted in the warmth of His light and love. I truly pray you make the right decision for not only yourself but also the ones who love you.

I have a scar on my upper left arm today from that very frightful night. I could have let that scar be a symbol of agony and let it turn into bitterness inside my soul, but because I gave everything to Jesus and declared I was not going to let go of Him, that scar is a symbol of how God has made me an overcomer and has brought great victory into my life. Give Jesus your scars, whether they are visible or invisible. He will make you an overcomer too.

The very first step in your journey to depending on God is receiving Jesus to be your personal Savior and Lord. This may be your very first time or this may be a reconnect time, but I encourage you to make it right between you and Him.

Jesus died on the cross for our sins. He did this so He could spend eternity with us. He wants to start now. He wants an intimate relationship with you. It was exciting when a lady I counsel with told me she recently received a revelation that Jesus wants to be her companion.

This is so true. She had been an active member of her church. She knew that Jesus died for her, but this I feel is the true beginning of a blessed relationship with God. God wants an intimate relationship with each one of us. He desires for us to share all of our life with Him on a daily basis.

The Bible declares:

> **9 if you confess with your mouth the Lord Jesus and believe in your heart that God has raised Him from the dead, you will be saved. 10 For with the heart**

one believes unto righteousness, and with the mouth confession is made unto salvation.

Romans 10:9-10 (NKJV)

Let us pray together:

Lord Jesus, I confess I have sinned against You. Your word states in 1 John 1:9 that when I confess my sins, You are faithful and just to forgive my sins and cleanse me from all unrighteousness. I receive Your forgiveness right now. I thank You for forgiving me and giving me a new beginning. I receive You as my Saviour and Lord. Take total control of my life. I thank You that I will live eternally with You forever, starting right now. You are my constant companion.

In Jesus' name, Amen.

If you cannot pray this prayer at this time, I encourage you to ask the Lord to reveal Himself to you through His Word. I ask you, whether you prayed this prayer or not, to read the book of John in the Bible. The Lord Jesus is a gentle shepherd. He loves you just the way you are. He wants only your very best and He knows you better than you know yourself.

He has a great plan for you if only you will surrender to Him.

Secondly, are you handling your grief on your own or are you depending completely on your Daddy God's strength? If you're not depending on Him, can we pause right now and pray a prayer for you to surrender to Him? He is waiting lovingly and patiently. He wants to carry you through this pain and grief.

> *Lord Jesus,*
>
> *I am so heartbroken and wounded. I have been acting like a child who prevents their parent from seeing their wound. I come now and hold out my hands and ask You to take me in Your loving arms. Hold me through this journey of grief. The Word states You are my husband. I now lean completely on You, depending on that promise. I am so thankful I do not have to do this alone. In Jesus' Name, Amen.*

Our Father, who art in Heaven, hallowed be Thy name. Thy kingdom come, Thy will be done on Earth as it is in Heaven. Give us this day our daily bread and forgive us our debts as we forgive our debtors. Lead us not into temptation, but deliver us from evil. For thine is the kingdom and the power and the glory forever. Amen

For I Know The Plans

The beloved hymn *"Solid Rock,"* written by Edward Mote, sums up the message of this chapter.

My hope is built on nothing less Than Jesus' blood and righteousness.
I dare not trust the sweetest frame,
But wholly trust in Jesus' Name.

Refrain

On Christ the solid Rock I stand,
All other ground is sinking sand;
All other ground is sinking sand.

(When darkness veils His lovely face,)
When darkness seems to hide His face,
I rest on His unchanging grace.
In every high and stormy gale,
My anchor holds within the veil.

His oath, His covenant, His blood
Support me in the whelming flood;
When all around my soul gives way,
He then is all my hope and stay.

When He shall come with trumpet sound,
Oh, may I then in Him be found;
Dressed in His righteousness alone,
Faultless to stand before the throne.

AMY BIRCHFIELD

These next two verses are not found in a typical hymnal, but when I researched the writer of this hymn I found out that he wrote two verses that indeed described even better the feelings I had.

My hope is built on nothing less
Than Jesus' blood and righteousness;
'Midst all the hell I feel within,
On His completed work I lean.

I trust His righteous character
His council, promise, and His power;
His honor and His name's at stake,
To save me from the burning lake.

On Christ the solid Rock I stand,
All other ground is sinking sand;
All other ground is sinking sand.

I truly believe, with my whole heart, God has a very special place in His heart for widows and orphans. I felt so many times a special grace and favor on my life after I lost Raymon.

The following Bible verses are just a few explaining how God feels about orphans and widows.

> **Religion that God our Father accepts as pure and faultless is this: to look after orphans and widows in their distress and to keep oneself from being polluted by the world.**
>
> *James 1:17 (NIV)*
>
> **The LORD protects the foreigners among us. He cares for the orphans and widows, but he frustrates the plans of the wicked.**
>
> *Psalm 146:9 (NLT)*
>
> **He administers justice for the fatherless and the widow, and loves the stranger, giving him food and clothing.**
>
> *Deut. 10:18 (NKJV)*

"Do not take advantage of a widow or an orphan. If you do and they cry out to me, I will certainly hear their cry.

Exodus 22:22-23 (NIV)

Loving my life as an officer's wife at one of our many military balls

CHAPTER V

Identity Crisis

Not only did I lose Raymon to Heaven, but also I lost my entire life as I knew it. My life had been completely absorbed by the military, and I had focused most of my attention on Raymon.

We had been in Atlanta for only a short time before Raymon went home to Jesus. I did not have enough time to put any roots down. The only people I knew were the ladies of PWOC and my friends at the military chapel.

All of my family was in Virginia. My sole focus was being the president of PWOC along with being Raymon's wife. Ever since Raymon and I started dating in May of 1998, I loved being on Raymon's left arm and witnessing the many times he saluted soldiers with his right hand. I loved being an officer's wife.

Even with all of its challenges and struggles, I loved being an officer's wife. I remember telling my sister shortly after Raymon and I started dating how I was dating an army officer. She immediately said, "Amy, you were created to be an officer's wife." I agreed. Now that Raymon was in Heaven my whole world had changed forever. That change happened in a moment.

Life can change so quickly. I know a lot of you can identify fully with this statement.

I was no longer an officer's wife. With all of my grief, I could not fulfill my role as president of the PWOC and I was alone in an Atlanta suburb. Yes, I had said I wanted my space and privacy when I was surrounded by people in Germany, but this was ridiculous.

I was granted a benefits package that I would continue to receive as long as I stayed a single woman. It was my severance package. It was as if the government said, "Thank you very much and now have a good life." I was sent on my way. I was so very thankful for this blessing, but truly I would give it all back if I could just have my Raymon.

I lost my husband, I lost my military family, and I lost my ministry. I felt I had lost everything and everyone that meant anything to me. The only one I had by my side was my Daddy God. Unfortunately, whether it is the total truth or not, I felt all of the friends that I did have no longer wanted to spend any time with me because I was now "single." I also felt that if it didn't have anything to do with me being single, it was because I was an instant "don't want to be around her in case this bad luck rubs off on us" case. I sometimes felt like I was too much of a burden for people to take on in their life. The very thing I had dreamt about the night before I left for Virginia for my dad's birthday had happened. People were too busy to stop their routines and their agendas to minister to my desperate need. Whatever it was, I went from being a respected major's wife to a nobody.

God's Perspective

I am not sure what identity crisis you may be going through, but I know that in your loss and your own personal tunnel, there is more than likely an identity crisis you are facing.

When we experience any kind of loss of great magnitude, our lives feel so shaken and uncertain. We experience a storm of the soul. I truly felt as if a huge hurricane mixed with some horrific tornadoes swept through my life the morning I lost Raymon.

What I truly believe will help us through these times is seeing what God's perspective is for us personally. You see, God doesn't want us to have our identity in anything or in anyone. He wants us to be grounded completely in Him. I believe so strongly this is paralleled in the parable of The Wise and Foolish Man found in the Bible:

> **[24] "Therefore everyone who hears these words of mine and puts them into practice is like a wise man who built his house on the rock. [25] The rain came down, the streams rose, and the winds blew and beat against that house; yet it did not fall, because it had its foundation**

> **on the rock. ²⁶ But everyone who hears these words of mine and does not put them into practice is like a foolish man who built his house on sand. ²⁷ The rain came down, the streams rose, and the winds blew and beat against that house, and it fell with a great crash."**
>
> *Matthew 7:24-27 (NIV)*

You see, if we have our identities built on anyone or anything other than Jesus we are building our lives on sand. When the storms of life come and beat upon our lives we will crash, but if we have our identities built on Jesus and who He says we are, the storms will come and beat on us, but we will not crash because our lives are built on the rock of Jesus Christ.

The enemy of our souls would love to whisper in our ears, "Your life is over. What you invested in or the person you invested your heart and life in is gone. Your life has been wasted, and it is all gone." He is a liar. The Bible states he is the father of all lies.

I experienced the pain of believing I invested my heart, life, and soul in Raymon, and I invested so much in my ministry with military families and women, and in one second it was all gone. The truth is this: not one second of one minute of one hour is wasted. God will use everything you did invest for good in some way.

The Bible says:

²⁶⁻²⁸ Meanwhile, the moment we get tired in the waiting, God's Spirit is right alongside helping us along. If we don't know how or what to pray, it doesn't matter. He does our praying in and for us, making prayer out of our wordless sighs, our aching groans. He knows us far better than we know ourselves, knows our pregnant condition, and keeps us present before God. That's why we can be so sure that every detail in our lives of love for God is worked into something good.

Romans 8:26-28 (The Message)

God put on my mind and heart a memory of Raymon telling me the last month he was with me that I was the reason he was so close to the Lord. Raymon acknowledged the Lord when we got married, but his faith was zero. He was open and honest about this fact, and his honesty was one of the many things I appreciated about Raymon. He never played games with anyone including God. He was truthful about where he was in every aspect of life.

When Raymon told me I was the reason he was so close to the Lord, it meant everything to me. He could not have told me anything greater. I was not the perfect wife and I failed many times, mostly with my attitudes and saying things I wish I had not said.

The enemy would taunt me saying, "You didn't do this and you didn't do this." I would come back with, "Yes. I may not have done that, but the most important thing is he is in Heaven."

Another part of our grieving is many times the loss of the dream of what would have been. This is very difficult as well. I know! Raymon and I had many plans and dreams. Back when we were dating, I could see us being together till we were in our golden years. We even joked often throughout our marriage about how he would chase me in his wheelchair with me on my walker. How he would be my eyes because of his great eyesight and I would be his ears because of how well I could hear. God will, if we allow Him, heal all of these hurts.

I do not know what your circumstance is right now, but do understand this: you can give it all to Jesus, and He is the only One who can make everything turn out right.

Who Are You?

First, I would love for you to listen to the song "Who Am I" by Casting Crowns.

Then please read the following Bible verses to soak in the truth of who you are. I recommend not only reading these verses through but also looking them up in different translations.

For I Know The Plans

WWW.BIBLEGATEWAY.COM is a fantastic resource.

You may find that the same verse translated in a different version may be easier for you to understand and speak to you in a very special way. Also, it will help the truth soak in more. Do not just read through them but really let the truth of God's word soak into your mind, heart, and soul. Write down the verses that really speak to your heart personally. Place them where you will see them to encourage you throughout each day.

Psalm 139:13-16 (NIV)

**13For you created my inmost being; you knit me together in my mother's womb.
14I praise you because I am fearfully and wonderfully made; your works are wonderful, I know that full well.
15My frame was not hidden from you when I was made in the secret place, when I was woven together in the depths of the earth.
16Your eyes saw my unformed body; all the days ordained for me were written in your book before one of them came to be.**

1 Peter 2:9 (The Message)

9-10 But you are the ones chosen by God, chosen for the high calling of priestly work, chosen to be a holy people, God's instruments to do his work and speak out for him, to tell others of the night-and-day difference he made for you—from nothing to something, from rejected to accepted.

Jeremiah 29:11 (NIV)

For I know the plans I have for you," declares the LORD, "plans to prosper you and not to harm you, plans to give you hope and a future.

Ephesians 1:4-5 (The Message)

3-6 How blessed is God! And what a blessing he is! He's the Father of our Master, Jesus Christ, and takes us to the high places of blessing in him. Long before he laid down earth's foundations, he had us in mind, had settled on us as the focus of his love, to be made whole and holy by his love. Long, long ago he decided to adopt us into his family through Jesus Christ. (What pleasure he took in planning this!) He wanted us to enter into the celebration of his lavish gift-giving by the hand of his beloved Son.

Ephesians 2:7-10 (The Message)

7-10 Now God has us where he wants us, with all the time in this world and the next to shower grace and kindness upon us in Christ Jesus. Saving is all his idea, and all his work. All we do is trust him enough to let him do it. It's God's gift from start to finish! We don't play the major role. If we did, we'd probably go around bragging that we'd done the whole thing! No, we neither make nor save ourselves. God does both the making and saving. He creates each of us by Christ Jesus to join him in the work he does, the good work he has gotten ready for us to do, work we had better be doing.

Ephesians 2:10 (NIV)

For we are God's handiwork, created in Christ Jesus to do good works, which God prepared in advance for us to do.

Psalm 139:1-4 (NIV)

¹ You have searched me, LORD, and you know me.

² You know when I sit and when I rise; you perceive my thoughts from afar.

³ You discern my going out and my lying down; you are familiar with all my ways.

⁴ Before a word is on my tongue you, LORD, know it completely.

Colossians 2:13-15 (The Message)

¹¹⁻¹⁵ Entering into this fullness is not something you figure out or achieve. It's not a matter of being circumcised or keeping a long list of laws. No, you're already in—insiders—not through some secretive initiation rite but rather through what Christ has already gone through for you, destroying the power of sin. If it's an initiation ritual you're after, you've already been through it by submitting to baptism. Going under the water was a burial of your old life; coming up out of it was a resurrection, God raising you from the dead as he did Christ. When you were stuck in your old sin-dead life, you were incapable of responding to God. God brought you alive—right along with Christ! Think of it!

All sins forgiven, the slate wiped clean, that old arrest warrant canceled and nailed to Christ's cross. He stripped all the spiritual tyrants in the universe of their sham authority at the Cross and marched them naked through the streets.

John 1:12-13 (NASB)

¹² But as many as received Him, to them He gave the right to become children of God, even to those who believe in His name, ¹³ who were born, not of blood nor of the will of the flesh nor of the will of man, but of God.

Galatians 4:6 (AMP)

And because you [really] are [His] sons, God has sent the [Holy] Spirit of His Son into our hearts, crying, Abba (Father)! Father!

1 Samuel 16:7 (NKJV)

But the LORD said to Samuel, "Do not look at his appearance or at his physical stature, because I have refused him. For the LORD does not see as man sees; for man looks at the outward appearance, but the LORD looks at the heart."

John 15:15 (NIV)

I no longer call you servants, because a servant does not know his master's business. Instead, I have called you friends, for everything that I learned from my Father I have made known to you.

Romans 5:1-2 (AMP)

Therefore, since we are justified (acquitted, declared righteous, and given a right standing with God) through faith, let us [grasp the fact that we] have [the peace of reconciliation to hold and to enjoy] peace with God through our Lord Jesus Christ (the Messiah, the Anointed One).

² Through Him also we have [our] access (entrance, introduction) by faith into this grace (state of God's favor) in which we [firmly and safely] stand. And let us rejoice and exult in our hope of experiencing and enjoying the glory of God.

Colossians 3:12 (NIV)

Therefore, as God's chosen people, holy and dearly loved, clothe yourselves with compassion, kindness, humility, gentleness and patience.

Galatians 3:26-27 (NIV)

²⁶ So in Christ Jesus you are all children of God through faith, ²⁷ for all of you who were baptized into Christ have clothed yourselves with Christ.

Psalm 138:8 (NLT)

The LORD will work out his plans for my life—for your faithful love, O LORD, endures forever. Don't abandon me, for you made me.

1 Thessalonians 1:4-6 (NIV)

⁴ For we know, brothers and sisters loved by God, that he has chosen you, ⁵ because our gospel came to you not simply with words but also with power, with the Holy Spirit and deep conviction. You know how we lived among you for your sake. ⁶ You became imitators of us and of the Lord, for you welcomed the message in the midst of severe suffering with the joy given by the Holy Spirit.

Romans 8:14-15 (NIV)

¹⁴ For those who are led by the Spirit of God are the children of God. ¹⁵ The Spirit you received does not make you slaves, so that you live in fear again; rather, the Spirit you received brought about your adoption to sonship and by him we cry, "Abba, Father."

Colossians 3:3-4 (The Message)

³⁻⁴ Your old life is dead. Your new life, which is your real life—even though invisible to spectators—is with Christ in God. He is your life. When Christ (your real life, remember) shows up again on this earth, you'll show up, too—the real you, the glorious you. Meanwhile, be content with obscurity, like Christ.

Ephesians 2:19 (NIV)

Consequently, you are no longer foreigners and aliens, but fellow citizens with God's people and members of God's household,

1 Thessalonians 5:5 (NIV)

You are all children of the light and children of the day. We do not belong to the night or to the darkness.

Philippians 3:20 (NIV)

But our citizenship is in heaven. And we eagerly await a Savior from there, the Lord Jesus Christ.

Hebrews 3:12-14 (The Message)

12-14 So watch your step, friends. Make sure there's no evil unbelief lying around that will trip you up and throw you off course, diverting you from the living God. For as long as it's still God's Today, keep each other on your toes so sin doesn't slow down your reflexes. If we can only keep our grip on the sure thing we started out with, we're in this with Christ for the long haul. These words keep ringing in our ears: Today, please listen; don't turn a deaf ear as in the bitter uprising.

2 Corinthians 1:21-22 (NIV)

Now it is God who makes both us and you stand firm in Christ. He anointed us, set his seal of ownership on us, and put his Spirit in our hearts as a deposit, guaranteeing what is to come.

1 John 3:1 (NIV)

See what great love the Father has lavished on us, that we should be called children of God! And that is what we are! The reason the world does not know us is that it did not know him.

Matthew 5:14 (NASB)

"You are the light of the world. A city set on a hill cannot be hidden;

1 Corinthians 3:16 (The Message)

¹⁶⁻¹⁷ You realize, don't you, that you are the temple of God, and God himself is present in you? No one will get by with vandalizing God's temple, you can be sure of that. God's temple is sacred—and you, remember, are the temple.

Romans 6:18 (NIV)

You have been set free from sin and have become slaves to righteousness.

1 John 5:18 (NIV)

We know that anyone born of God does not continue to sin; the one who was born of God keeps him safe, and the evil one cannot harm him.

2 Corinthians 5:17-21 (NIV)

¹⁷ Therefore, if anyone is in Christ, the new creation has come: The old has gone, the new is here! ¹⁸ All this is from God, who reconciled us to himself through Christ and gave us the

ministry of reconciliation: ¹⁹ that God was reconciling the world to himself in Christ, not counting people's sins against them. And he has committed to us the message of reconciliation. ²⁰ We are therefore Christ's ambassadors, as though God were making his appeal through us. We implore you on Christ's behalf: Be reconciled to God. ²¹ God made him who had no sin to be sin for us, so that in him we might become the righteousness of God.

Ephesians 2:6 (NIV)

And God raised us up with Christ and seated us with him in the heavenly realms in Christ Jesus,

I pray these verses will be used in your life to raise your head up to Jesus. He will day by day reveal more and more to you through His word and the Holy Spirit. He is the lifter of our head.

Yes, we will grieve the loss of our precious loved one, and yes, we will grieve the loss of who we were because of this person, whether we are no longer a wife, husband, daughter, son, sister, brother, friend, or whoever else we were.

The sooner we stand on the rock of Jesus Christ as our all in all and we make our relationship with Christ our eternal identity, we will overcome. This does not erase the pain, but it will keep the enemy of our souls from tormenting us with his lies. Please do not try to fill this huge gap of who you are now with anything or anyone else but Jesus Christ.

Just like the man who built his house on the sand, if we try to fill our great loss with anything else or anyone else, it will not work. It will be another temporary fix, but your house will eventually crash again. We can take only so many of these crashes. Please make your identity sure on the rock of Jesus Christ. He is the same yesterday, today, and forever. He is faithful, and no matter how much the circumstances change, He remains to be the same loving Daddy God. He will never leave you or forsake you.

Child of God

If we believe in the Lord Jesus as our Savior and Lord, we are truly children of God. What God desires for us to know is He loves us, and He cares only about our relationship with Him. He does not want us to carry out our faith walk in some kind of religious way, but only trusting He is our Daddy God. He created you for relationship. He loves you unconditionally, and He wants the same from you. The more we truly step into this truth, the more and more we will stand firmly on the rock of Jesus Christ. We will be unmoved and unshaken no matter what comes our way.

Dearest Jesus,

I am so thankful for the gift of being a <u>(wife, husband, etc.)</u>. Please forgive me for placing all or part of my identity in my role as a <u>(wife, husband, etc.)</u>. I want you to be my all in all. I am so thankful You will always be with me. You created me in my mother's womb, and I was always supposed to be completely Yours. I surrender to Your will and Your word. I declare today that I am Yours and You are mine. In Jesus' Name, Amen

Widow Identity

Something I want to caution you about is taking on the widow or widower identity. This can also pertain to other kinds of losses. It is so easy to fall into that mentality. I knew in my heart I did not want to have my identity wrapped up in being a widow. Yes, you will get attention when you explain to someone that you are a widow. This is more likely for the younger widows. Unfortunately, people are not surprised when senior citizens inform others that they are a widow or widower for understandable reasons.

Regardless, even at that age they can be challenged not to take that on as their identity. The biggest payoff for taking this on as our identity is the attention we receive from others and the self-pity we feel internally. Neither of these is Christ centered. Yes, we are allowed the grieving period, but even in this we should not take on this grief and new status as our identity.

I personally did not like the fact that I felt like a total killjoy in conversations when I entered a room. I felt like the perpetual bummer. I would be in a great conversation, and then the person would ask what brought me to Georgia. I would say that it was my husband, which would ultimately lead me into telling them what happened. Then would come the "Oh, I'm so sorry" with the very sad face. Hence, the killjoy.

Jesus desires to be the center of our hearts and lives. We are to glorify Him. Instead of us taking all of the attention for ourselves, we should be testimonies of what God is doing in and through our lives. What a light we can be and an encouragement if we would only choose not to wrap our identities in being a widow, widower, or any other great loss and instead live in the identity of Christ. I talk more about what that can look like in Chapter 11.

Dawn has always been my guardian angel

CHAPTER VI

People Within Our Tunnel

I called my sister the Chief of Staff during the first days I was home after Raymon went to Heaven. She took on the responsibility of deciding where things needed to go, what needed to be cleaned or vacuumed, and who did what. She did not have a problem delegating any responsibilities.

One of the things I learned about people was the way they all wanted to help in some way. In fact, the chaplains and all of the PWOC ladies were fighting over who was going to do what even before I arrived home from Virginia. Everyone's love was sustaining for the first ten days.

I was so thankful for my friends that were with me the day I came home to my empty house. After I visited Raymon's room and saw the bed where he breathed his last breath, I came downstairs. My friends were sitting at my dining room table waiting to spend time with me. I set Raymon's picture on the table and was comforted looking at his sweet smile.

The chaplain had brought elements for communion. He had thought of me earlier that Sunday morning, and he didn't want me to miss out. It was so appropriate to share communion with my caring church family. They were indeed being the body of Christ to me. This was so unexpected but so beautiful.

An Unexpected Visitor

I had many questions for the Lord. Some people feel they cannot ask God questions. This is a false belief. The Lord wants us to have a relationship with Him. He wants us to keep the dialogue going, especially when we are traveling on our rough roads in life. One of my many questions was "Who is going to be my protector now?" He answered this question pretty quickly.

My sister, my mother-in-law, my friend Jen, and I came home from dinner after running errands. This was my first day back on Monday, March 5. I was sitting on the loveseat when I started shaking from head to toe. I heard everything around me, but I could not respond to anyone. My sister threatened to call 911 if I did not respond.

As much as I wanted to, I could not respond. I heard my sister talking to the 911 operator. I could not believe this was happening. Next thing I knew, this police officer came walking into my den and stood as though he was at attention, facing me on my left side. The paramedics came in and surrounded me. They took my blood pressure and checked my blood sugar levels. I still could not communicate with them. Then

I heard the head paramedic say, "Get a stretcher and an IV started." It took all I had but I got the word "No" out of my mouth.

Everything seemed to calm down. My sister explained to them that I had just lost my husband. They responded with, "We know. We are the ones that came to the house to assess the situation with her husband." I was able to ask them questions. They sat next to me and explained what they saw. They said, "It was a calm and peaceful situation."

When they left, the police officer was still standing in the same spot. He waited till all the paramedics were gone, then he asked if he could sit next to me. He took my hand so gently and said, "I know you are in a lot of pain right now, but everything is going to be OK. I am from California. My son and I moved to Georgia after my wife was involved in a tragic car accident and was killed by a drunk driver."

He understood my pain and encouraged me that all would be well. He told us, "My name is Gabriel." The moment he told us his name, the room was full of awe. I knew God had answered my question. He was letting me know He had people in place to protect me. Gabriel told me he would always be looking around my house to insure all was well. In the days ahead, Gabriel made frequent visits to insure I was indeed OK.

Ministry of Presence

Family and friends visited over the next few days. We had a lot of planning to do. My mother-in-law and I respected each other and worked so well as a team. She confided in me, "I promised Raymon I would be here for you if anything happened to him." She did just that.

It meant so much when my friend Suzanne drove out from Texas. We were stationed together in Germany. She drove 950 miles on a moment's notice to be with me. She was there making my favorite sandwich, and she was holding me close the morning of the funeral. She was there in the midnight hour.

I remember when we went to our local pancake house. I looked at her and asked, "What am I going to do now? We just bought this house, and now I am alone here in Georgia." She did not answer me because she did not have an answer. She could do what she could do and no more.

The bottom line is that people do not have the answer. They will try to do what they can, but this is a very difficult situation for people to know exactly what to do. For most people, dealing with other people's loss is scary and uncomfortable. People hate feeling uncomfortable. They will do almost anything to escape any situation in which they feel they don't know what to do or say. You will be surprised who shows up and who does not.

The first question most, if not all, of my friends asked when I broke the news that Raymon went to Heaven was "What can I do?" I know it will probably be very hard at first for you to think of something, but try to give them a specific thing to do to help. I frankly had a very hard time doing this. Down deep, I just wanted someone to show up. I have a difficult time asking friends for help. I am aware of all of their responsibilities, and I don't want to add to their list of burdens. My friend Jen was wonderful. She did what may have seemed like a very simple thing, but it meant the world to me. She brought me a brand new very soft robe and body wash. She said that she wanted to give me something that would bring me some comfort. It was perfect! It doesn't take much. Communicate with your friends that little things like this example would mean a lot.

If you are like me, your true friends really do want to be there for you, but they really do need your help and permission to do those things. For example, if you are having a difficult time doing a specific chore, ask them to please help you with it. If you are having a hard time getting up in the morning, ask one of your friends to please call you at a specific time and encourage you. If you have children, ask them to give you a couple of hours in the evening once a week to go do something for yourself. My point is, be specific and help them to help you. Don't be embarrassed or feel as if you are a burden. You really will make their day giving them something to do to help you.

The funny thing about me thinking I didn't want to be a burden to my friends was that they were thinking the same thing about themselves. They didn't want to be a burden to me.

The ministry of presence is the most important thing we need at this time. We all know there are no words to say or that we really need to hear or want to hear right now. If you do want someone to simply be there for you, try asking them to have a scheduled coffee date with you once a week. You could also invite them over for a movie night. Don't be shy about telling your friends that you would just like them to be with you. Let them know they don't have to try to say something. There isn't anything to say sometimes. Just their being with you is comforting enough.

Abandonment in the Tunnel

On my journey through this tunnel of loss, I have found out more about people than at any other time of my life. My experience may differ from yours, but I have a feeling this may bring some light to some of the situations you may encounter.

The Garden of Gethsemane

> **36 Then Jesus came with them to a place called Gethsemane, and said to His disciples, "Sit here while I go over there and pray." 37 And He took with Him Peter**

and the two sons of Zebedee, and began to be grieved and distressed. ³⁸ Then He said to them, "My soul is deeply grieved, to the point of death; remain here and keep watch with Me."

³⁹ And He went a little beyond them, and fell on His face and prayed, saying, "My Father, if it is possible, let this cup pass from Me; yet not as I will, but as You will." ⁴⁰ And He came to the disciples and found them sleeping, and said to Peter, "So, you men could not keep watch with Me for one hour? ⁴¹ Keep watching and praying that you may not enter into temptation; the spirit is willing, but the flesh is weak."⁴² He went away again a second time and prayed, saying, "My Father, if this cannot pass away unless I drink it, Your will be done." ⁴³ Again He came and found them sleeping, for their eyes were heavy. ⁴⁴ And He left them again, and went away and prayed a third time, saying the same thing once more.

⁴⁵ Then He came to the disciples and said to them, "Are you still sleeping and resting? Behold, the hour is at hand and the Son of Man is being betrayed into

> **the hands of sinners. ⁴⁶ Get up, let us be going; behold, the one who betrays Me is at hand!"**
>
> *Matthew 26:36-46 (NASB)*

Jesus, in the garden of Gethsemane, was dealing with what I believe was the hardest thing He had to face on this earth. He was about to die on the cross for you and me. He was about to take on all of the sin of the world past, present, and future. The disciples were just far enough away to give Him some space. He was crying out in agony to Father God to the point that He was sweating drops of blood. When He walked over to His disciples, they were fast asleep. He asked them, "Could you not stay awake one hour?" They had in a sense abandoned Jesus in His darkest time.

One thing is necessary during this year and beyond as you are traveling through your tunnel. We need to keep a heart of grace and avoid being bitter. You may have even been hurt by someone by the time you read this. I encourage you to forgive that person and set them free from any demands. I so wish I could tell you I didn't wrestle with this, but I did. I was so hurt, and I didn't understand why people would not be by my side in my darkest hour. Didn't they know I was going through the worst time in my life? I was all alone.

Jesus, in the garden, prayed a prayer of "Not my will but yours be done." Set people free and no longer look to them to meet your needs. Look to God and watch Him do amazing things.

God Encounters

He sent me Elijah, my neighbor, who lives three houses down from me. He was faithful in helping me with my yard and other things around the house. Even my mailman, Michael, was a very sweet man that smiled every time he brought me my mail. I even had an unknown man that would play beautiful trumpet music every day at noon behind my house in the parking lot where he worked. God brought me my Waffle House family. They were my new friends who faithfully enjoyed coffee and breakfast with me. I met people everywhere who were so kind and loving.

You will be so blessed and ready for these new encounters when God brings them to you. Just let go of your expectations of people. You will be so blessed with peace, and you will know God is your helper and husband. He knows your needs and knows how to meet them better than any person you may have known for years.

I was so blessed with a God encounter that truly surprised me. I had called the Detective that I spoke with the morning Raymon went to Heaven. I asked her if there was any way she could visit me and go over what had happened that terrible morning. Not only did she come to my house, but she brought her supervisor. I was expecting the story of the facts, but they gave me more than I could have imagined. They were both Christians, and they loved on me and encouraged me. The detective walked me through what happened: how they entered the house and how they found Raymon in his bed. One huge thing that she said that gave my heart comfort was that Raymon's room was full of peace. She told me that she has had to deal with many terrible things, but entering that room was a place of peace. When we came back downstairs, both of the women took my hands and prayed for me. It was one of the most beautiful surprises God granted me. (This same detective ended up being a longtime friend to my current sister-in-law, Heather.)

People may encourage you to attend grief counseling groups in church. I encourage you to go. Even if you do not stay throughout the weeks, you may find a friend that you can do things with that knows what you are going through.

Relationships

For those who are dealing with a loss of a wife or husband, relationships are new things to face and deal with. I was encouraged by close friends not to date for the first year. I had no intention or desire to date. I could not understand why some men paid attention to me so soon after my husband's death. In fact, I had someone hit on me before my husband was laid to rest. This was very shocking.

I did meet someone within the first year after Raymon was gone. He was so kind and attentive. I was so lonely and missed the companionship and help a man can offer. He got my attention when he asked, "Do you feel the church is doing what they are called to do for a widow?" I honestly felt at that time they were not. He wanted to be there. He did help me with a lot of things around the house and with my car. He was a great companion.

My strong suggestion here is to be very careful. This time you are walking through is a very vulnerable time. Have in place strong boundaries, because your feelings right now cannot always be trusted. Trust your boundaries. I highly recommend you meet the person at a neutral location. You might meet at a restaurant or movie. If you do not feel peace, do not proceed forward.

God will let you know. Listen to Him. Please do not listen to the lie that says you have no one else. Do not settle for people in your life that are not healthy to be around. Trust God even though another loss is very hard to deal with now.

This man I mentioned before, I believe, was placed in my life for a particular season. He was not God's long-term plan for my life. It is so important to know when to let go. I feel I did hang on too long. I encourage you to trust God and let go when you know He is saying to let go.

There may be people who will be drawn to you because they feel superior. They love feeling as if they can be the hero in a situation. We need to ask God to give us discernment as to who these people are.

There are organizations that will help you do almost anything you need to have done. Again, trust

God and try to listen to the Holy Spirit. Listen for warnings. FOLLOW PEACE!!!

It is so important to surround yourself with uplifting people. No negative Nellies and negative Nelsons. I highly recommend the book *Boundaries* by Dr. Henry Cloud and Dr. John Townsend. Step by step, it will help you know how to deal with people and how to have healthy boundaries. We need to have healthy boundaries when it comes to every area of our lives.

If you take this approach with people, you will be at peace within yourself. If hurt feelings do come because of people, take the hurt immediately to the Lord.

Cast your cares on the LORD and he will sustain you.

Psalm 55:22 (NIV)

As you do this, the Lord will show you He has you in His hands and will indeed meet your specific need(s). Tragedy and loss have a way of showing you who your true friends are. Not only that, you will meet people that you would have never met otherwise. I have met some beautiful treasures of friends because of my tunnel of loss. God "Bless The Broken Road" that led me to these precious ones.

Cloud of Witnesses

We cannot make this journey on our own. When I came home from D.C., I was still dealing with thoughts of ending my life, but they were not the horrific feelings I had felt in my hotel room. In this part of my tunnel, I felt feelings of utter darkness and extreme loneliness. I missed Raymon so much. Raymon and I shared a deep dependency on each other in our marriage. In military life, you move around a lot. This makes you even closer. From the very beginning, Raymon and I had such a deep bond. We truly were best friends, and I loved him more than anyone I have ever loved in my life.

He was my safe place in this crazy world. He was the first one to offer me a secure life and home. We were truly there for each other in the good and bad. I felt with Raymon gone that half of me was missing. Do you want to know what kept me from ending my life? It was Raymon. God used Raymon in my life again, even when he was in Heaven.

I knew without a shadow of a doubt if I did end my life, he would have looked at me with a very disappointed look. He would have said something like, "Amy, why? You had such an important purpose to fulfill on your journey. I told you the best was yet to come. So many people are going to miss out on the things you had to offer." I knew he would have been downright upset with me, and I wanted him to be happy and proud of me. What he thought and said meant everything to me. He believed in me so very much.

If you are experiencing extreme darkness in your tunnel and feel you want to end this journey. Know this— you have an important purpose left to fulfill. I know it doesn't feel like it right now. I know things are very dark. We need to keep moving forward in the tunnel to see the light. Please trust me when I say the light is ahead. Your precious loved one wants nothing more than for you to complete your life's journey. Their journey is over on this earth, but yours is not. If you can't do it for yourself, do it for him or her. Make them proud. You have a purpose here that only you can fulfill. Your beloved is in your cloud of witnesses and cheering you on. I believe they would be sending a message like the one Rascal Flatts sings in "My Wish".

> **Therefore, since we are surrounded by such a great cloud of witnesses, let us throw off everything that hinders and the sin that so easily entangles. And let us run with perseverance the race marked out for us,**
>
> *Hebrews 12:1(NIV)*

Dear Jesus,

I want to first thank You for all the people You have given to me in this time of grief and sadness. I pray many blessings upon them. I now bring You my expectations of people. I want so badly for people to know what to say and do. I know they are going to naturally fall short of this. There are so many reasons why they cannot. Lord, my focus needs to be on You. You are my source and comfort. I trust You to take care of all of my needs. Lord, I have been hurt by _____. They have let me down. I release them into Your hands. I no longer hold a grudge and I ask You now to forgive me for anything I have held against them. I forgive them. I pray that You will bless them. My hope and expectation is in You alone. Thank You in advance.

In Jesus' Name, Amen.

Chapter VII

Forgiveness Brings Freedom

My friends were not the only ones I had to forgive. There were so many different areas and people in my life I had to release to God. In this chapter, I will cover about most of my tunnel experiences dealing with forgiveness and my journey through it. I hope this chapter brings some light to some areas you may be struggling with on your journey. I will be sharing about the hardest struggles I had in battling bitterness and overcoming through forgiveness.

I was instructed, by God, to open up about this part of my heart when we had a missionary come to our church from Israel. He spoke to us about the feeding of the five thousand. He shared how the disciples wanted to send them on their way and let them get their own food. Jesus instructed them to feed them. His main message was to love everyone.

This missionary lives in an area where the Arabs and the Jews are very separated in all ways concerning their daily lives. The missionary spoke a great truth. God loves everyone and has instructed us to love everyone. Jesus did not die for one people group. He died for every single human.

AMY BIRCHFIELD

Our Enemies

My husband died because of the effects of the war in Iraq. He was there for a year. He was in Baghdad, and his base was bombed on a daily basis. The bombing was a constant occurrence. Raymon told me how they would be in their cafeteria and would hear the squeal of the incoming bomb. Everyone would just stop for a moment and see where it landed. When they saw they were still alive, they would move on with the business of eating. I can't imagine this kind of existence. On one of our calls, I heard a lot of commotion and Raymon quickly told me, "I have to go. I love you." They were anticipating an incoming bomb. I had to sit there with the phone in my hand wondering if that was the last time I would ever speak to Raymon. It was absolutely terrifying.

When Raymon came home to me, thankfully, on July 11, 2004, I had no idea what I was about to deal with. Every single night for two straight years, he had nightmares and what we called "episodes." He had PTSD (Post Traumatic Stress Disorder). The last six months of his life were the worst.

When Raymon had his first daytime episode at work, it was absolutely devastating. His captain informed me of what happened later that day when we met in the emergency room. He said Raymon was sitting at his desk when he started to scream, "Incoming! Incoming!" At first, Raymon tried to get under his coworker's desk for cover. When that didn't work, he grabbed his backpack and flew onto the floor so as to hunker down for cover.

Up to that time, Raymon and I were the only ones that knew what he had been dealing with. That day everyone became aware of our internal struggle. The Iraqi terrorists who bombed my husband's base on a continuous basis are some of the people I needed to forgive.

Forgiveness in no way is saying we condone what a person or people have done. Forgiveness is releasing the people into God's hands. God truly is the only one who righteously and justly handles each and every situation. Forgiveness is giving every part of our hurt and bitterness to God and trusting Him to take care of us and the parties involved.

Anytime I struggle with forgiveness, I meditate on the passage found in Matthew 18:21-35.

> **21 Then Peter came up to Him and said, Lord, how many times may my brother sin against me and I forgive him and let it go? [As many as] up to seven times? 22 Jesus answered him, I tell you, not up to seven times, but seventy times seven! 23 Therefore the kingdom of heaven is like a human king who wished to settle accounts with his attendants. 24 When he began the accounting, one was brought to him who owed him 10,000 talents [probably about $10,000,000],25 And**

because he could not pay, his master ordered him to be sold, with his wife and his children and everything that he possessed, and payment to be made. [26] So the attendant fell on his knees, begging him, Have patience with me and I will pay you everything. [27] And his master's heart was moved with compassion, and he released him and forgave him [cancelling] the debt. [28] But that same attendant, as he went out, found one of his fellow attendants who owed him a hundred denarii [about twenty dollars]; and he caught him by the throat and said, Pay what you owe! [29] So his fellow attendant fell down and begged him earnestly, Give me time, and I will pay you all! [30] But he was unwilling, and he went out and had him put in prison till he should pay the debt. [31] When his fellow attendants saw what had happened, they were greatly distressed, and they went and told everything that had taken place to their master. [32] Then his master called him and said to him, You contemptible and wicked attendant! I forgave and cancelled all that [great] debt of yours because you begged me to. [33] And should you not have had pity and mercy on your fellow attendant, as

I had pity and mercy on you?[34] **And in wrath his master turned him over to the torturers (the jailers), till he should pay all that he owed.** [35] **So also My heavenly Father will deal with every one of you if you do not freely forgive your brother from your heart his offenses.**

Matthew 18:21-35 (AMP)

The Lord has forgiven me so many times and for so many sins. There is no way I could hold any unforgiveness towards anyone. Plus I know that He will handle my enemies in the perfect and holy way. I truly believe God loves everyone, and the way He handles each and every situation ultimately is for the good of that person and hopefully to lead them to salvation and freedom in Him. If it was up to us we would send them to Hell and have no compassion in our hearts. We want people to pay for the hurt and pain they have caused us and our loved ones. Thankfully, that is why God is God and we are not. God had mercy on us, and I am so thankful for this every day.

I recently heard a story about a man that is an enemy of the Christian faith and Americans. He was killed in a battle. Christian missionaries wanted to show him love and give him a proper burial. As they were carrying him to that place of burial God raised him from the dead. He told the people what God had shown him. God had shown him the pain and blood shed he had caused his victims, through their eyes, and allowed him to see Hell.

God loved him very much that he wanted him to see the truth of his life and the god that he was serving was really satan. He became a Christian. This story summarizes what I have just said about God dealing with each one in a way God only can and doing it in such a way that it brings that person to salvation and repentance. Release your enemies to the Lord. You will be set free.

The Doctors

After Raymon's episodes became public, the Army sent him to several doctors to see what the problem was. PTSD was not being treated very well at that time. Since my husband's death, there have been great strides in working with soldiers with these severe internal wounds. I am very thankful that they are being helped now with improvements. This is not to say that there are not soldiers out there that are struggling still to this day, but at least the treatment of soldiers struggling with PTSD is more of a priority.

When the doctors got involved, it was another whole battle. We were sent to a well-known neurologist in our town. He walked into the examination room with a big fat book. He sat down in a chair, put the book on his lap, and asked Raymon what were his symptoms.

Raymon began to tell him the situation. We told the doctor he had PTSD. The doctor immediately threw that diagnosis out the window and stated after just a couple minutes of sitting with us, "You do not have PTSD." I could not believe my ears.

The doctor listened to Raymon's description of his symptoms and thumbed through his book. He would ask Raymon questions, and they would go back and forth. Finally the doctor told Raymon, "You have epilepsy."

Again, I could not believe my ears. I told the doctor I had a problem with his diagnosis, and this made him irritated. He turned and walked right up to me with a very stern look on his face. He told me I was acting like a teenage girl who was told she is pregnant. He went on about that for a few minutes. I just sat there stunned. I left that office feeling violated, and Raymon's situation only got more stressful. I felt our time with this doctor was absolutely useless and harmful.

After our call to the scheduler, we no longer saw this doctor. They sent us to a couple of army doctors. They ran a series of ambulatory EEGs where Raymon had a bunch of wires on his head covered with bandages. The first one was worn for forty-eight hours. A month later another one was worn for eleven days. Watching Raymon wear that contraption on his head for eleven days was unbelievable. It was uncomfortable for him to sleep in, and sleep was something I believe he needed desperately.

Who would be able to sleep with the mere discomfort of having a hundred wires on your head wrapped up in bandages while expected to have an episode? I found it horrific watching my sweet Raymon have to endure all of it. He was such a champion. He was so meek and didn't complain. I respected him so deeply for his tremendous courage through all of it.

He did not have one single episode when the EEG apparatus was on his head. What was so bizarre was that each time it was taken off, Raymon ended up having a terrible episode and seizures.

For example, we had to drive to the north side of Atlanta for his appointment to take the bandages off. After his appointment, we went to the mall to relax and enjoy some part of the day. I was sitting in a massage chair in one of the stores. It was so relaxing. Raymon was ready to go, but I asked if he could give me another minute. Suddenly, Raymon made a sound and he went down to his knees right in front of me. He had a full-blown episode followed by seizure activity. My legs were blocked by the weight of his body. I just held on to him and prayed.

The paramedics came and checked him out, but by the time they got there, the worst was over. When they asked if I wanted them to take him to the hospital, I told them no. At this point we were so exhausted with all of the stress, and his case was being overseen by a couple of doctors already. Raymon was handling everything in great stride.

We had a meeting with Raymon's flight surgeon. Every aviator has their own. We both sat in his office to discuss the situation. He looked at me sternly after I told him that Raymon's PTSD was due to his tour in Iraq. He said, "We cannot be certain this is from his tour." I clearly stated to him, "Well, since my husband was healthy when he left me, and this is the state in which he came home to me, what do you think?" He did not reply.

We had to go to Augusta to see an Army neurologist, which required a two-hour drive both ways. They tasked different Army soldiers with driving us to these appointments. The doctor said he could not find anything wrong after his MRI. He also told him if he did not have an episode for a month, he would give Raymon his driving privileges back.

I was pleasantly surprised when Raymon went a month with no nightmares and no episodes. It appeared he was getting better. We went back to his doctor a month later, and Raymon could not wait to tell him the good news. The doctor informed Raymon he still would not be able to drive, and he could not carry a gun. Raymon had asked the doctor specifically about a shooting club he wanted to be a part of and the answer was "no." My husband had been a soldier for twenty-five years and was an expert shooter, yet he could not carry a gun. I sat there and watched Raymon receive the news that he could no longer do two things he loved to do. I sat there and watched my husband put his head into his hands and watched as life was draining out of him. The joy was being replaced with great despair.

It was not long after this appointment that my husband went home to the Lord. I felt the doctors did absolutely nothing to help and actually made the stress unbearable.

Raymon's flight surgeon came up to speak at the funeral. He sobbed openly. He shared with everyone how he had not realized how very serious Raymon's condition was. I believe he knew I could have hurt him so badly with accusations. He could see instead forgiveness and compassion in my eyes. He told everyone how I was ministering to him more than he could ever minister to me. We embraced when he came down from speaking.

Yes, I did forgive him. I saw the sorrow from him, but the Lord very gently nudged me on several occasions to forgive the other doctors. God worked on my heart layer after layer. Sometimes forgiveness and healing are like that. Our journey with God is a learning and growing process.

It wasn't until my mom ended up in the emergency room that I would finally and completely let go of my bitterness towards the other doctors.

My parents moved down from Virginia in December 2010. The Georgia air had an effect on my mom's health, and I was so concerned about her because of her labored breathing. It had been a very long time since she had dealt with any episodes of her asthma. The concern was so great we had to call an ambulance. I was by my mom's side the whole time in the hospital. I walked out to the nurse's station to ask a question. Suddenly, I was faced with Raymon's first neurologist, the man who had violated me with his awful accusations.

He didn't see me, and if he did, I doubt he would have remembered me. Four years had passed since that awful visit. An awful gut-wrenching feeling was in my stomach. Honestly, I was saying to God in my heart, "Really, God. I am scared about my mom, and now I have to revisit this awful memory." But God knows what He is doing.

My mom was stable and just waiting for the fluids to do their job. My dad was with her. I walked out of the ER and went to the hospital chapel. It was a small room, but I felt the presence of God in this place. I cried out to God to help me to forgive. I didn't want to hold on to this bitterness in my heart.

It had been there for so long. I knew God wanted me to forgive, and He says in His Word if we do not forgive others, we will not be forgiven. I felt the Lord's presence and I just cried, "Please help me!" I wanted to have love and peace in the place of bitterness. I heard His voice tell me to turn to Psalm 51.

I opened the hospital chapel's Bible to this passage and I read it aloud.

AMY BIRCHFIELD

¹ Have mercy on me, O God,
according to your unfailing love;
according to your great compassion
blot out my transgressions.
² Wash away all my iniquity
and cleanse me from my sin.
³ For I know my transgressions,
and my sin is always before me.
⁴ Against you, you only, have I sinned
and done what is evil in your sight;
so you are right in your verdict
and justified when you judge.
⁵ Surely I was sinful at birth,
sinful from the time my mother
conceived me.
⁶ Yet you desired faithfulness even in
the womb; you taught me wisdom in
that secret place.
⁷ Cleanse me with hyssop, and I will be
clean; wash me, and I will be whiter
than snow.
⁸ Let me hear joy and gladness;
let the bones you have crushed rejoice.
⁹ Hide your face from my sins
and blot out all my iniquity.
¹⁰ Create in me a pure heart, O God,
and renew a steadfast spirit within me.
¹¹ Do not cast me from your presence
or take your Holy Spirit from me.

For I Know The Plans

¹² Restore to me the joy of your
salvation and grant me a willing spirit,
to sustain me.
¹³ Then I will teach transgressors your
ways, so that sinners will turn back
to you.
¹⁴ Deliver me from the guilt of
bloodshed, O God, you who are God
my Savior, and my tongue will sing of
your righteousness.
¹⁵ Open my lips, Lord, and my mouth
will declare your praise.
¹⁶ You do not delight in sacrifice, or
I would bring it; you do not take
pleasure in burnt offerings.
¹⁷ My sacrifice, O God, is a broken
spirit; a broken and contrite heart
you, God, will not despise.

Psalm 51 (NIV)

Now some of you may be thinking, "What did she do? The doctors lacked wisdom in their care, and she lost her husband. She has the right to be mad." This attitude will keep you in bondage forever. Father God knew what the doctors had done. He will take care of each and every one of them. God commands us to forgive no matter what the wrong may be. It is not a suggestion but a commandment.

> **For if you forgive people their trespasses [their reckless and willful sins, leaving them, letting them go, and giving up resentment], your heavenly Father will also forgive you.**
>
> *Matthew 6: 14 (AMP)*

I felt peace and wholeness when I walked out of that chapel. Father God did not make us to hold resentment in our souls. I am so glad I finally forgave. I did not have to deal with the ugly reality of bitterness any longer. Now I ask you this question: Is there anyone you need to forgive?

Me

Another person I had to forgive was ~ME. When we lose someone, sometimes the "should'ves" or "could'ves" come to torment us. I dealt so severely with the "should'ves" for a long time. This pure torment was horrible, and the enemy of our souls loves it.

It took a long time for me to stop beating myself up for not seeing how serious things were. I knew Raymon was having a very difficult time, but I had no idea he was dying. In fact, as crazy as this may sound, after he went to Heaven I would look at several of his pictures in the last year of his life, and I would be mortified to see him look the way he did. At the time, I did not see it. I believe God must have veiled my eyes.

Looking back, I saw so many things I would have done or said differently. I asked Raymon several times before I left to see my family if he had peace about me leaving him. He would always say that he did. You see, I did not leave his side for a long time. I was his battle buddy. I took on the role of protector. I tried so hard to make his reality softer then it was.

An example of this occurred when we attended the Army Christmas Ball in Atlanta. I prayed we would not have any problems. Raymon wanted to make life as normal as possible, especially for me, despite the hell we were faced with. I prayed constantly, "Please, God, no episodes tonight."

The three hundred plus Army soldiers and their dates were all seated. We were ready for all the formalities the military has at each ball. The round of toasting began: to the Army, to the president, to the wives (soldiers/husbands stood up), and then we toasted to the Fallen Comrades.

There is always a single table set with symbolism at each formal ball. The soldier started to state what each piece of the place setting symbolized. It is a very emotional and honorable ceremony. This is when Raymon made a sound, and I knew it was bad.

I gently took the water glass out of his shaking hand, and slowly we went down to the ground. I knelt over him and tried to comfort him as best as I could. The chaplain ran over and placed his hand on Raymon's back. I looked up and quickly saw the most beautiful sight. Three soldiers were standing arm to arm to protect Raymon's privacy. They were our guardian angels.

After what seemed like several minutes, I slowly raised Raymon up and placed him in his chair. The water glass had sloshed around, so I cleaned up his area as if this incident had not happened. Even though it appeared Raymon was conscious, it would still be a few minutes till he was completely aware. I asked the people around us not to say anything about it. I waited for forty-five minutes before asking Raymon to walk me to the bathroom. We went into an empty meeting room, and I told him what had happened. He just nodded and acknowledged what I said.

I asked him if he wanted to go back to our hotel room. The ball was at a hotel, and we had booked the room for the night. He said no, we would still enjoy the evening. I had such respect for the way Raymon faced this terrible ordeal. We even stayed and danced the night away. I hope it was a great testimony to the God we served. We were not going to be defeated. It was only by God's strength we were strong.

Even though I did what I felt was the best I could with a situation I never dreamed of dealing with, I was still mad at myself for so many things. I was mad for leaving him to go to Virginia for my dad's birthday. I was mad for all the times I got stressed and said things I should not have said to him. I got really mad at him on our last Sunday together.

I was running behind for our chapel service and I had a lot of responsibility that morning. I was the lay person facilitating the whole service. I was also singing a solo. I knew I could not be late. I had to do all the driving. Our chapel was twenty-two miles away from our house.

I got so mad at Raymon because I did not feel he was helping me get my things together. I am a typical woman when it comes to getting ready and usually it takes a lot longer for us to get ready. I just wanted Raymon to get my Bible and purse so we would be able to run out the door when I came downstairs. I was on edge all the time because I never knew when he would have another episode, and they were so scary. I was dealing with Secondary PTSD. I went off and began to let my stress out on Raymon. He plugged his ears and asked me to stop, but I could not stop my mouth. I asked the Lord to please forgive me for blowing it. I looked and sounded like a lunatic. I was an emotional mess all the way to the chapel. Then I had to get in front of everyone to lead them in worship service. In fact, I honored Raymon for his birthday that was the following day.

We went to lunch after the service. I asked him to forgive me. He did, and he added, "We need to start getting ready for church on Saturday." I agreed, and all was well. There were no more Saturdays for us. He was gone on Friday.

I got us involved in square dancing classes shortly after we arrived in Atlanta. He told me he was very tired, but I wanted so badly for us to have fun and enjoy life. I thought it would do us good and let us relieve some stress. We would have our lesson, and he would just have to sit. I would ask him to dance, but he just said, "I'm too tired." I would pout. I had no idea how exhausted he was.

These are things I thought about after he was gone. I so wish I had known how bad it was. I had no idea he was dying. I would have made sure he had everything that he needed and more. I would have taken him anywhere he wanted to go. I would have told him how much I appreciated him and how thankful I was for him being in my life. God used Raymon in my life to bring such healing and just be the best friend I have ever had.

What is it you wish you had done or said, or not done or said? These things also need to be forgiven. I know that God and your loved one would not want you to continue being bitter and angry at yourself. Release the "should'ves" and "could'ves" to the Lord. They do no one any good. In fact they will absolutely drive you utterly mad. God wants to grant you His peace.

God gave me a wonderful dream one night. I do not know whether it was entirely a dream or a gift from God. "In my dream" I went into Raymon's room and he was lying there. I poured out my heart to Raymon. I told him everything I wanted to say—how sorry I was and how much I loved him. It felt so real. In fact, in the dream he lay down, and I told him I wasn't done yet. He sat back up and listened to me. He had a tear running down his sweet face. I woke up from this dream and felt such a release in my soul and heart. I know Raymon knew my heart and loves me still, more perfectly than ever before.

God?

Are you mad at God? Oh, you should have seen me when I got the call telling me the news Raymon was gone. I was yelling at God to resurrect him. I was not saying please. I was mad at God for leaving me alone.

Later in my tunnel, I would take my fist and pound on Raymon's bed. I would tell God, "You said in your word it *is not good for man to be alone*. What is this?" God truly wants you to tell Him how you really feel. He wants you to be free to share your most intimate feelings. He can handle it. He would much rather you and He work out your relationship than to see you moving farther and farther away.

He is your Daddy God. When you work through the awful bitter feelings there will be a beautiful deep relationship waiting for you and Him on the other side. It was years before I realized I still had not fully forgiven God. In fact, during my quiet time with Him, He revealed to me I was still holding on to those hard feelings, and it was coming out towards the people around me. I wanted to be totally and completely free. I wrote in my journal Daddy God, I – Forgive – You. When I wrote those words, there was a huge release in my whole being. I felt the enemy was finally defeated in this area. I felt God's love flood over inside of me.

I knew I had truly finally let go. Again it is a layer by layer process we walk through, especially with severe situations.

Our Loved One

Lastly, are you mad at the one who is gone now? Sometimes this may not seem logical. Feelings are not always logical. Then again, there may be some real logical reasons why you would be mad. This is okay to admit as well.

Some of my reasons really did not make sense. We were supposed to get our house in order in March. We were going to get rid of items we didn't need. When I looked at all the mess I had to deal with alone, I was upset. It is true you do not take one single item with you when you die.

I was upset that Raymon had not fulfilled his promise to me in Germany. He was going to give me a great thirty-fifth birthday. It was the first birthday back in the States for a few years. May 10 came around and it was an awful day.

I was upset that he didn't tell me how bad things were for him. Looking back, I truly believe he knew. I know he must have been dealing with many of his own feelings. I wish he would have told me. I would have had the chance to make sure we did some very special things together. I would have accomplished some important things.

There could be some leftover business you did not get to resolve between the two of you. It is perfectly acceptable to admit you are mad at the person who is no longer with you. It is how you deal with it that matters.

I suggest you write a good long letter to your loved one. Tell them how you feel. Ask the Lord to help you let go and release those things to Him. Another way to release your hurt and anger is to talk to him or her—like the effective counseling tool using an empty chair. I had something very recent come up in my soul that I had never dealt with. Raymon and I had never resolved it completely. I let my feelings out. I let Raymon know how I felt. I then forgave him. Place a chair in front of you and have a talk. Let your feelings out and say those powerful words "I forgive you". I pray you will feel the same release I did in my soul and heart.

Let me pray with you:

Dear Jesus,

I ask for You to forgive me for holding these bitter and angry feelings against You, others and myself. I ask You to walk with me through the road of forgiveness and healing. I trust You to take care of those I feel wronged my loved one and me. I release them to You. Replace this anger and bitterness with Your peace and love. I love You.

In Jesus' Name. Amen.

(I also encourage you to pray the prayer in Psalm 51 and listen to Matthew West's song "Forgiveness".)

Chapter VIII

One Day At A Time

Therefore do not worry about tomorrow, for tomorrow will worry about itself. Each day has enough trouble of its own.

Matthew 6:34 (NIV)

I could not even think past each day. I was just handling the things that were in front of me. The Lord created a morning and an evening to set apart each day from the other. He made us to carry no more than what one day would bring us. The routine of life was very daunting, and I found it impossible to think of the next day much less the next evening.

When you enter into your tunnel of loss, you may find things that came easy to you before will be difficult. For example, I had been very good at keeping a budget, and after I entered my tunnel, it was so hard to even keep the bills paid on time.

It is natural for us to wonder and even worry. A common question people ask in the tunnel is, "What are we going to do now?" All of the plans I had envisioned for my husband and me were gone. The spring held many exciting things for us. We lived in an area where it was very easy to ride our bikes to restaurants and fun activities, and we talked about the different ideas we had in mind. We were so excited to be back in the United States after three years in Germany. We had a five-year time line planned.

When we moved to the Atlanta area, we had great hopes we would retire there. We bought our home on August 21, 2006. In fact, as I was writing this chapter, I realized today was the six-year anniversary of the purchase of our home. We were going to start a ministry, and we had a lot of ideas and plans. I did not realize our plans were not God's plans for us.

Pain in Perspective

Two months after we laid Raymon's body to rest in Arlington National Cemetery, I went to D.C. alone. It was our eight year anniversary and I wanted to see his new headstone. It was also Memorial Day weekend. While I was there, God led me to do something that helped me tremendously.

I was walking around the D.C. area when I saw the United States Holocaust Memorial Museum. I went into the museum and proceeded to take in the entire tour. At the end of the tour, I sat and listened to video testimonies from the survivors and listened intently to the accounts of their horrific experiences. I knew God was using this tour to help me get my pain in perspective. He wasn't nullifying my pain or my own experience. He was helping me to understand there are people who suffer as much or more than I did. This experience gave me extra strength and grace to go forward in my healing.

I would encourage you to go to a Holocaust museum near you. If you do not have one close, rent a movie depicting the true story of the Holocaust. Hopefully, you will see what I mean.

This very same day, my mom tried to be very encouraging through my tunnel. I say "tried" because she was limited in what she could do with the distance between us. She would encourage me with her calls. While I was visiting D.C., one of these encouraging calls came at just the right time. She called to relay a message from Daddy God. The message was this:

> **When you pass through the waters, I will be with you; and when you pass through the rivers, they will not sweep over you. When you walk through the fire, you will not be burned; the flames will not set you ablaze.**
>
> *Isaiah 43:2 (NIV)*

Starting Your Day Right

It is so important how we set our minds at the beginning of our day. I started each day at my special window saying good morning to Daddy God. I prayed

He would guide me and lead me that day. I prayed He would fill me with His love so I would make Him proud and pleased with me. I wanted to be a blessing to others. My prayer was found in the song by For King and Country "The Proof Of Your Love." This was and is my heart's desire. I so encourage you to have your own Daddy God time. Thank Him for each new day regardless of how you feel.

I then read from my devotional. I would journal what I received from the Lord, my thoughts and prayers. It is so important to journal your true feelings, especially now. When you experience God's revelations to you, it will truly encourage your faith. I would encourage you to get devotionals that speak on grief and the valley experience. A great place to read in the Bible is Psalms, where David cried out to God and found encouragement for his soul.

Thanksgiving raises our hearts, souls, and heads out of despair. Thank God for the simplest things and watch that list grow and grow. This alone will help us out of our doldrums. It is so easy to fall into the pit of despair, especially when we allow ourselves to complain and bicker about things. Every time we complain we are digging ourselves into our own pit. When you read the Psalms, you will notice that David talks about his problems and complains about the people and situation, but then he allows the Lord to encourage his heart. He begins to praise the Lord and he talks about all the things he is thankful for. It is okay to be honest with the Lord about how we feel, but don't stay there. Allow the Lord and also yourself to stir up that encouragement and begin to praise the Lord for Who He is and all the things He has blessed you with.

Daddy God blesses us more and more when we choose to be thankful. It is just like an earthly parent dealing with their child. If you give blessings to your children and they complain and bicker about what they have, a parent's heart does not say, "Let me give you something else to complain about." You don't want to give them anything, but if they are thankful and appreciate all that they have, you want to give them more and more. Daddy God is the same way. Indeed our Daddy God has given us so much more than what we deserve because of His great grace and love, thus God is pleased when we choose to be thankful. We will also have hearts of joy because we are grateful.

Complaining can be more dangerous than just making us feel down; it can lead to us making very poor choices. All throughout the Old Testament there are so many examples of how the children of God were serving the Lord with gladness and then started complaining and bickering about their situations or people. The next thing you know they go off and make very poor choices that God is not pleased with at all. He withdraws His hand of blessing, and they start receiving the consequences of their behavior and choices. They become miserable, and then they come running to God knowing they were rebellious and stupid. They beg God to forgive them, and out of His mercy and great love He restores them to Himself. They are good for a while until they again start complaining and bickering about what is happening. Instead of turning to the Lord for His help, they go make another mess.

Please keep this in mind as you travel through your tunnel of loss. Daddy God has everything you need. Please turn to Him and only Him and be thankful for whatever He blesses you with, and you in turn can be a blessing to others.

Worry About Nothing, Pray About Everything

I learned the above title and saying in my youth group at Liberty Baptist Church in Hampton, Virginia. It was a very short paraphrase of the verses found in Philippians 4:6,7 (NIV)

> **⁶ Do not be anxious about anything, but in every situation, by prayer and petition, with thanksgiving, present your requests to God. ⁷ And the peace of God, which transcends all understanding, will guard your hearts and your minds in Christ Jesus.**
>
> *Philippians 4:6,7 (NIV)*

Be still and know I am God. These are the words the Lord spoke to me right before I received the official word my husband was with the Lord. These are words He wants you to receive. Worry is the opposite of trust. Trust our Father God. He is trustworthy, and great is His faithfulness! Worry is really a cousin of fear that opens the door for the enemy. Whatever we continue to feed our souls by way of our thoughts will become more powerful in our lives. We have a choice to choose worry or trust. When our feelings want to dwell on fear or worry, let our mouths speak words of faith.

Words kill, words give life; they're either poison or fruit— you choose.

Proverbs 18:21(The Message)

Speak words of faith and see how the Lord will respond.

The Bible makes this truth about worry very clear in Matthew 6:25-34 (NIV)

Do Not Worry

25 "Therefore I tell you, do not worry about your life, what you will eat or drink; or about your body, what you will wear. Is not life more than food, and the body more than clothes? 26 Look

at the birds of the air; they do not sow or reap or store away in barns, and yet your heavenly Father feeds them. Are you not much more valuable than they? ²⁷ Can any one of you by worrying add a single hour to your life? ²⁸ "And why do you worry about clothes? See how the flowers of the field grow. They do not labor or spin. ²⁹ Yet I tell you that not even Solomon in all his splendor was dressed like one of these. ³⁰ If that is how God clothes the grass of the field, which is here today and tomorrow is thrown into the fire, will he not much more clothe you—you of little faith? ³¹ So do not worry, saying, 'What shall we eat?' or 'What shall we drink?' or 'What shall we wear?' ³² For the pagans run after all these things, and your heavenly Father knows that you need them. ³³ But seek first his kingdom and his righteousness, and all these things will be given to you as well. ³⁴ Therefore do not worry about tomorrow, for tomorrow will worry about itself. Each day has enough trouble of its own.

Matthew 6:25-34 (NIV)

<u>Letting Things Go</u>

One day at a time also pertains to the process of letting things go. When I saw all the things that Raymon had left behind, it was so overwhelming. I was embarrassed when our ten big crates of stuff arrived when we moved into our new Atlanta home. We had no children to blame it on either. We were it. We were two people with a whole lot of stuff. We were so excited about how we were going to simplify our lives by selling or donating many of our items. When Raymon went to Heaven in March, I felt abandoned to do that big job all by myself. What a way for someone to get out of a job! Of course, I am being lighthearted when I say this.

What I am about to share with you is something I learned from Raymon. Raymon helped me with my storage unit shortly after we started dating. I felt conflicted on what I should keep and what I should let go. He encouraged me concerning some of the items. He would say, "Hold on to it. When it is time you will let it go." My advice to you is the same. Hold on to it and when the time is right you will let it go. There may be items you are ready and willing to let go. Then there may be items you just can't imagine being without. When it is time, you will let it go. Let go of the items you can do without and go on with life. It will happen. There is a season for everything.

One of the items I had a hard time letting go of was Raymon's uniform. On the last night of his life,

Raymon laid out his uniform to wear the next day. It was lying at the end of his bed as usual. When I saw his room for the first time after he passed away, I was so moved by it. It was just like Raymon to be prepared.

It was a reminder that he was prepared to live the next day, but it was a day he did not see, not here on earth anyway. I left his uniform there for about seven months. I just could not move it. I always remembered the lesson that Raymon taught me. "When it is time, you will let go."

There was also a picture of Scooby Doo on his wall. He absolutely loved Scooby Doo, as I mentioned in the first chapter. A friend had given me a beautiful stone block wall hanging that said "Beautiful Reunion." When it was time, I replaced Scooby Doo with that hanging. It was another letting-go process.

My recommendation to you is this: try to take one item a day and decide what to do with it. Do you want to give it to a family member? Do you want to donate it? Do you want to sell it? There are options. You can also have a special footlocker or chest just for special items. There will be a time for you to let go. Do not feel you need to push yourself to do it. Do not feel as if you have to do something that someone else wants you to do. This is your personal tunnel to take one day at a time.

There are situations that may not give you a choice and a luxury of time. Do the best you can. If you have to get a storage unit in the meantime, that is a great temporary fix. Try to make the situation as simple as you can possibly make it. Do not be afraid to ask for help.

Be strong and courageous. Do not be afraid or terrified because of them, for the LORD your God goes with you; he will never leave you nor forsake you."

Deuteronomy 31:6 (NIV)

You see, no matter what you are faced with each day, the Lord is with you!

Father God,

I want to thank You that I can trust You. I do not have to be worried or afraid. You have me in the palms of Your hands. Absolutely no one or nothing can snatch me out of them. Father, forgive me for the times I have allowed my mind to stay in the grips of worry. I place my life and all of my needs in Your hands. Whenever I am tempted to worry, I will speak Your name, Jesus. I will lean on Your everlasting arms. You say in Your Word to come as a little child with simple faith. Thank You for being my Daddy God, my provider.

In Jesus' Name. Amen

Be Still, My Soul

1 Be still, my soul: the Lord is on thy side.
Bear patiently the cross of grief or pain.
Leave to thy God to order and provide;
In every change, He faithful will remain.
Be still, my soul: thy best, thy heav'nly Friend
Through thorny ways leads to a joyful end.

2 Be still, my soul: thy God doth undertake
To guide the future, as He has the past.
Thy hope, thy confidence let nothing shake;
All now mysterious shall be bright at last.
Be still, my soul: the waves and winds still know
His voice Who ruled them while He dwelt below.

3 Be still, my soul: when dearest friends depart,
And all is darkened in the vale of tears,
Then shalt thou better know His love, His heart,
Who comes to soothe thy sorrow and thy fears.
Be still, my soul: thy Jesus can repay
From His own fullness all He takes away.

4 Be still, my soul: the hour is hast'ning on
When we shall be forever with the Lord.
When disappointment, grief, and fear are gone,
Sorrow forgot, love's purest joys restored.
Be still, my soul: when change and tears are past
All safe and blessed we shall meet at last.

5 Be still, my soul: begin the song of praise
On earth, believing, to Thy Lord on high;
Acknowledge Him in all thy words and ways,
So shall He view thee with a well-pleased eye.
Be still, my soul: the Sun of life divine
Through passing clouds shall but more brightly shine.

                              Kathrina von Schlegel (1697-1797)
                                             (public domain)

CHAPTER IX

Time-Out

It is vitally important for your mental and emotional well-being to take time-outs from pain and grief. There are a few ways to accomplish this.

<u>*An Activity to Escape*</u>

One way to take a time-out is to choose an activity which allows your mind to think of nothing but that activity. This activity should be something you love to do. You would absolutely laugh at one of my time-out activities: it was computer games. Go ahead and laugh! Yes, it is what people would say is a total waste of time, but it worked for me.

Before I met Raymon George, I did not even know what a computer game was. I am kidding to an extent, because I had played solitaire on my previous computers. Raymon was a genius on computers. He actually built his own. I remember walking in his office for the first time and seeing all his games. I have to admit I was a little concerned.

In our marriage, I would be jealous of him playing his games for a long period of time instead of being with me. It was in a sense his escape. I was not aware of how this escape was so important to him at the time.

Now do not get me wrong. I think any activity can be completely out of balance and can become excessive. This is wrong and very harmful to us and our relationship with others.

The activity I recommend for your time-out should be a personal, solo activity, one you can do alone and still enjoy. I just want your mind to be totally into that activity. Please do not feel that it is a waste of time or that you are being selfish. It is for your own sanity that you take a break from reality and not feel any demands on you. It is your therapy!!!

Some examples of time-out activities are:

- Computer gaming (a certain social network has quite a few cute, simple, and fun games)
- Sewing (please make sure it is something that will allow you to escape from demands and memories)
- Renting movies (preferably funny and light hearted)
- Running/walking
- Drawing
- Painting
- Sculpting
- Making jewelry
- Logic puzzles, Sudoku, crossword puzzles, fill-ins
- Origami
- Reading

The Need for Touch

One important part of my therapy, especially in the first year, was receiving massages. Yes, it is therapy in several ways. First of all, it is so important to have the ministry of touch. This need goes unfulfilled, especially when we lose a spouse.

It is well documented that if a newborn baby is untouched while the other needs are being met, they will die. We need touch. I know some of you may need touch more than others, but it is still a vital need that needs to be met in our lives for us to be healthy.

The way I met my need for touch was through massages. I personally asked for a female massage therapist at an affordable and classy salon. It was truly a blessing. Shop around and do not be afraid to ask questions. Some of your friends may be able to recommend a massage therapist for you.

Massage therapy does not have the same stigma it once had. In fact, it is well recognized for its healthy results. Again, do not feel guilty or feel that you are being selfish. I say go as much as you can afford and your time allows. The first year I went on a weekly basis because of the prices being so affordable.

Some of the benefits of massage are:

- Decreased anxiety
- Enhanced sleep quality

- Greater energy
- Improved concentration
- Increased circulation
- Reduced fatigue

Those who receive massages often report a sense of perspective and clarity after receiving their massage. The more massages you have, the better you will feel, but do not be surprised what one massage can do for you.

I have met several women that say because they are self-conscious about their bodies, they will not go for a massage. I want to encourage you. I am in no way a model-perfect shape. I have never felt at any time a sense of judgment by my therapist. I have always felt accepted for who I am and what I look like, with or without smooth legs.

The benefits stated above far outweigh any concerns you may have. Please do not feel self- conscious about your self-image or how you may react while in the massage.

I have talked to several massage therapists over the past several years, and they are ready for anything that happens in the room. In fact, I had the honor and blessing of counseling a massage therapist. She loves to minister to her clients by listening to them, but this brings about compassion fatigue. I shared with her to take each burden to the Lord after each of these clients. She said it changed her life, and she continues her ministry to her clients.

Do not be surprised if you cry while receiving your massage. It is only a way for your soul to cleanse and release those emotions. Massage therapists are very aware of this. If you do not have a good experience with your therapist, there are so many other therapists to choose from. Please try again because it is worth it.

Another great way to fill this need is by being a hugger. When you see a friend or family member, hug them. It has been said that receiving eight hugs a day keeps us healthy. Also you will be a blessing to whomever receives that hug. I just caution you, please use wisdom, especially whenever you are dealing with the opposite sex. My rule of thumb when I hug the opposite sex is, it is always safe to do the side hug. Always respect others' feelings. There are people that for whatever reason do not hug or who feel it is not appropriate. If you go for a hug and they stick out their hand to shake yours, shake their hand.

Take Time-outs to Nap

After your massage, you may want to take a nap. Naps are vital to your "time-out" regimen in the midst of your tunnel. Naps are very healthy to take for our bodies and minds. Now your nap does not have to be long. Your nap can be as short or as long as you personally need it. It does not have to be the same amount of time every day either. For me, I can sometimes lie down for fifteen minutes and get up and feel great. Other days I will nap for an hour or more. The most important thing is to listen to your body. It will tell you what you need.

There is a wide spectrum of beliefs when it comes to napping. Some of your families may have felt napping was a sign of laziness. Others were raised in families like mine where napping was a normal occurrence. It is reported that people that take the time to rest in the afternoon live longer and are healthier people. In fact, when you take a nap, not only will you not be lazy, but also you will feel more productive if you feel rested. Stress wreaks havoc on your body, and sleep is a great way for your body to heal.

If you work outside the home, lie down and take a power nap when you get home. It will make for a more enjoyable evening. It will help ease a stressful day you may have had. If you take a short nap, it should not interrupt your sleep at night.

Go to Bed

Go to bed at a regular bedtime. One big mistake I made was failing to do this. For some reason I would stay up way too late almost every night. It really made me feel tired the next day. I've heard experts say that you have healing sleep anytime you go to bed before midnight. I truly believe them. When we are tired, we tend to make the emotional journey even harder to handle. Our judgment is off, and this makes for poor decision making. We can be irritable. This does not help when we are trying to keep the friends we have. We feel sluggish overall. So please take this advice and go to bed.

You may feel going to bed at a decent time is easier said than done. A suggestion to help you get in the bed is to set an alarm for your bedtime. Go to bed when the alarm goes off. There are several other things you can incorporate in your life to help you achieve a good bed-time or sleep. One, have a night-light if you can't stand the dark. Second, have a fan or sound machine to block out all the different noises. Third, invest in a home alarm system. They are actually fairly inexpensive. There is a lot of competition out there that you can shop and get a good price. In fact, they will place a new one in your house for free so they can get your business. Having an alarm system helps with feelings of insecurity.

Fourth, get an animal if you do not already have one. They are a great source of comfort and companionship. I highly recommend, if you shop for one, to make sure their temperament suits yours.

Fifth, make sure you do not eat or drink anything that would prevent good sleep. I know this varies among people. I know that a good cup of milk or soothing tea helps many. Sixth, read a good book, such as books that have inspirational messages. I truly love the short-story books. Of course the Bible is a great way to end the day as well.

Let's pray:

Dear Jesus,

Thank You for the opportunity to rest my mind and soul. Show me the things I can do to do this. Lord, please direct my steps to find the right massage therapist. I thank You for the gift of touch and the ministry it provides. I pray You will help me go to bed when I need to rest. Thank You for designing me to heal, body and soul, while sleeping. Lead me through this journey I pray.

In Jesus' Name, Amen.

CHAPTER X

Maintaining Life

This chapter covers important nuggets of wisdom about your physical, emotional, and financial well-being, which are a vital part of our overall health. When you take care of the following things, you will be ready to go forth and live a healthy life when you come out of your tunnel, and I believe with all of my heart, you will.

PHYSICAL WELL-BEING

Before I begin this section, please understand that I am not a professional. I am sharing with you a plan that I felt led to do and how it has changed me. Please always get the approval of your doctor before you start any program that affects your well-being.

When we are walking the road of grief, our reactions to food may vary. For example, some may avoid food, and some may overindulge. The first couple of weeks after Raymon's passing I did not eat much at all, and later I did not care what I ate. I was in survival mode.

I gained a total of eighty-six pounds traveling through my tunnel. I do not believe I drowned myself with food, but I simply took an "I don't care anymore" attitude. I did not care how I looked. I felt I did not have anyone to look good for so why bother?

Since my husband was a soldier, he was very conscious of body image. He was also conscious of my body image. This was good in one way because it kept me motivated. So when he was gone, I felt as if absolutely no one cared, and neither did I. This attitude did not help me in the long run. As I became more and more healed emotionally, the gained weight remained. In fact, I am still trying to overcome those extra pounds.

My encouragement to you is this: Do not try to diet during the first year but do be conscious of your weight. Don't do what I did, and that was to totally be unaware of where I was presently on the scale. Be mindful!!! This is not the time to put extra pressure on you. Now I keep track of my weight on my notepad next to my scale, and it is my measuring stick. The scale is not there to beat you up, but only to let you know from day to day or week to week when to cut back a little bit. That is it!!!

As far as what I eat, no food is off limits. Rather, I try to use moderation. When I see I have gained, I cut back sweets and fried food for the day. I use my scale as the measuring tool.

When I was ready to lose the extra pounds, I struggled to find the way to get out of the black hole of weight gain. I did try different things for short spurts but I would fail. I was so scared, and I did not want to gain anymore. I wanted to be free of my grief weight. I prayed and cried out to Daddy God for help and He heard my cry. He gave me His plan, and it is the way I will live for the rest of my life. Let me share it with you, and if you need help too I pray it will be what brings you victory in this crazy battle of extra pounds.

Sundays are my official weight day. I start every week with whatever the number on the scale is on that day. For example, if the number is two hundred fifty on Sunday, then this is where I start. Sunday is also my free day. I can eat whatever I want, and I do not exercise that day.

Monday I weigh myself first thing in the morning after I greet Daddy God with a "Good morning" and "I love you." I keep things in perspective. Monday is usually always a gain day because of my freedom the day before. On my gain days I have predetermined exercises that I choose from. These exercises are golf and tennis on warm days, and on cold days I work out on my game system for an hour doing aerobics. These are very good exercises for me to guarantee a pound loss.

I also drink nothing but water on those days and eat no bread and sweets after breakfast. I weigh myself every morning, and what that scale says determines what exercise I am going to do that day and how I will eat.

On days that I stay the same weight I work out with my walking video for thirty minutes. I allow myself a little more freedom with eating but still try to be conscious of it. On days that I have a loss, I work out with my video game system that includes activity movement. I allow myself a treat on these days, such as a fast-food ice cream cone or something similar. When I have a loss during the week I crumple up my paper that I put my starting weight on for that week and use my new number for the rest of the week. At the completion of the week on Sunday, my weight becomes the official weight loss or gain number.

I have a big notebook in which I record the week number, the starting weight for that week, and the weight I am on that particular Sunday. I usually have a gain on the weeks I call my winter (menstrual cycle week). This God plan has worked so well for me because it keeps things interesting and I never feel deprived. I relate it to traveling down the road and if you see a gain you slow down and if you lose you can speed up a little bit. I have lost an average of a pound a week and will do this for the rest of my life. Let me chart out this plan in a different way that may help you.

- Pick the day of the week that is your start day and free day
- Write down your weight on a pad of paper
- Pick the three different exercises you will do for each:
  - Gain day (The most calorie-burning exercise you can do)

- - Maintain day (Exercise that will last thirty minutes at a moderate level)
  - Loss day (An activity that is fun but makes you move)
- Weigh yourself every morning before eating
- Based on your official weight day, decide what exercise and eating plan you will choose for that day
- Eating:
  - Gain day (Water only for beverage and no bread or sweets after breakfast)
  - Maintain Day (Limit bread and sweets to one)
  - Loss day (Be free but not as free as a free day)
- Track your official weight each week in a notebook

Learn from your gain days and move forward with that knowledge. In fact, what I do is look at my day before when I have a gain day and pick one thing I will eliminate or change. I have seen my eating lifestyle get healthier and healthier with these choices. Each person is different from another and each person can react differently to various foods. This is your personal journey. Grow in knowledge and use that knowledge to win the victory. If you have any questions please feel free to e-mail me.

It is important to always start with a fresh new beginning each week. Leave the past in the past and move forward. This will help you continue on a good path. Please celebrate each and every victory you have. Conquering each pound is truly something to celebrate! There are many things we can do to celebrate without consuming food. I personally just celebrate with joy that I am moving forward to my ultimate victory in health and wellness.

Water is vitally important!!! Make sure you drink at least eight cups of water daily. No matter how you have to dress it up, the important thing is to consume it. I drink only bottled water, but do your own research to see what is the healthiest. I like water regardless of the taste. My challenge is being mindful of drinking the water. I have to set my alarm every hour to remind me to do it. Another suggestion is to carry your favorite water container with you wherever you go. Do what works for you. I know that some of you do not like the taste of water, but here are a few suggestions to help. Use lemons, limes, oranges, or strawberries to bring wonderful flavor to your water. Furthermore, use a crystal glass; then you will be drinking your water exactly like the women and men do at expensive spas.

Exercise is so important during our time in the tunnel. It helps you release negative emotions and will help you gain positive clarity. It will help you with your energy levels and is a great way to maintain social connection. When I started, I wore my husband's running shoes. I felt him cheering me on.

My instructor, Diane, was very encouraging. She helped me be a part of her class. When I didn't show up, she would drop me a postcard saying she missed me. Having a wonderful instructor like Diane will help immensely with your exercise experience.

The important thing is to find some activity that you love to do. When we hear the word "exercise," we immediately groan inwardly. There are many ways to accomplish your exercise goals during the week.

You can walk. Choose a place you will be safe and experience the wonderful surroundings of God's blessings. If you live in an area where you do not have a nice place to walk, or you do not want to walk outside, there are wonderful instructional DVDs focused on walking. This is also a great way to get your walk in when the weather is not suitable for you to be outdoors.

You can go to a gym, and this is highly recommended if you want to be around people. It also may be a great blessing to hire a trainer at the gym. A trainer can help you stay motivated and accomplish goals you may have.

If you are like me, bored easily with exercise, I have an idea to share with you that helped me tremendously. Take several options listed below that you would enjoy doing. Write each one on a piece of paper and place them in a bowl. Pick one daily and do that particular exercise. Feel free to replace these with exercises that you personally enjoy. This will keep the exercises new and interesting.

Exercise options:
- ❖ Walking
- ❖ Running
- ❖ Swimming
- ❖ Gym (Weight Training)
- ❖ Gym (Cardio Training)
- ❖ Exercise class
- ❖ Tennis
- ❖ Bike Riding
- ❖ Bowling
- ❖ Volleyball
- ❖ Skating
- ❖ Water Aerobics
- ❖ Dancing (Play your favorite music and enjoy!)
- ❖ Golf

Also, you can list different workout DVDs on each paper and throw them into the mix. Whatever you do, enjoy it for a period of time that works for you. This exercise is not intended to be a burden but something that will make you feel better. Start out exercising twenty minutes a day and go from there. It is always better to start out slow and work your way up, and if you stay at twenty minutes consistently that is fantastic!

It is so important for your total well-being to get a physical. This will help your mind, body, and soul. When someone close to us is gone, it can start playing havoc with our minds. We may wonder how we are doing. Grief does things to our body that we may not understand. Go ahead and see a doctor that you trust. It is better to see a doctor sooner rather than later for a better sense of well-being.

Always have your concerns and questions written down for them. If you don't, you most likely will leave forgetting something you really wanted to ask or talk about. Do not wait to think of the questions when you are in the office. Feel free to ask or talk to the doctor about any concerns you have. I know it can be difficult sometimes to find a doctor you are comfortable with, but you can always continue to search for one.

My favorite doctor is my chiropractor. He has helped me tremendously with keeping my body aligned. He is so good that I see him only every four months on average. I am very modest about seeing my GP doctor. I believe if you can be healthy by regular chiropractor visits and good nutrition that is the best way to go. I personally would like to stay off of prescription medicines.

Before I entered into my tunnel, I had an awesome memory. In fact, people would be amazed at all the little details I could recall. While in my tunnel, I had the hardest time remembering simple things. This was very frustrating. Then I ran into another widow at the nail salon, and we struck up a wonderful conversation. She started laughing about something she could not remember, and then said, "Oh, my widow brain." There it was—my answer, finally. I asked her about her widow brain and she confirmed she also had a good memory until she entered her tunnel. I was relieved.

I thought for sure I had something major going on with me physically. Be encouraged if your memory is lacking. It is called Widow Brain.

EMOTIONAL WELL-BEING

Now let's talk about our emotional and mental well-being. It is so important to have someone to talk to about all the feelings we are experiencing. Ask your church if there is anyone they can refer you to. If you do not belong to a particular church, call a local church anyway. If you are a senior, ask your local senior center. I was blessed to have a counselor at Fort McPherson.

She was there whenever I needed to sit down and discuss all I was going through. Do not be discouraged if after a couple of times you don't find the counselor that is right for you. Try again. It is worth finding the right counselor. I am now doing lay counseling with women, and it is such a wonderful opportunity to share my experiences and training with others.

I also do inner healing prayer which is a prayer that I lead women through so they can hear what the Lord has to say directly to them. I have been counseled by a dear friend using inner healing prayer, and it has brought much freedom and healing. It is wonderful to use the same tool to share with others so that they can experience freedom and healing as well.

Crying was something I did a lot of, especially in my first year of loss. I would crawl up in my lounger and say to Daddy God, "Please, hold me." The Holy Spirit is our comforter. He will comfort us if we welcome Him to.

It is so healthy to cry. I feel God gave us this reaction to our sadness and grief as a blessing.

Every time I would cry, I felt a great release in my soul. It literally was a cleansing to my most inner being. Please do not feel bad or guilty for your tears.

We were all raised in different family settings where emotions ranged from not showing them at all to being very emotional. Crying is a very healthy emotion for men and women. If you end up crying in front of people, it may make others feel uncomfortable. This stems from their family of origin. There is a time to cry and to laugh. Trust God with your emotions. Ask Him to give you the freedom to express those emotions in a healthy way.

> **"I cry out loudly to GOD,**
> **loudly I plead with GOD for mercy.**
> **I spill out my complaints before him,**
> **and spell out my troubles in detail..."**
>
> *Psalm 142:1-2 (The Message)*

FINANCIAL WELL-BEING

It's funny that I would go from crying to finances. Your finances can make such a big difference in how you feel from day to day. My number one suggestion for you is to have a budget!!! It is so easy right now to buy things to make you feel better, whether that be food, clothes, knick-knacks, etc. We all know the pleasure of "retail therapy."

A budget will help take all the guesswork out of what you can afford and what you cannot. At first, it may be a total pain to come up with one. You will see that it takes out all the questions and stress of where you are. Just as the scale is a tool to keep track of your weight, a budget keeps track of your financial well-being. Do not let a budget scare you. It is simply taking your income and subtracting your monthly bills. The remaining amount can be placed in separate envelopes for gas, food, and entertainment. Some people do not like doing budgets because they simply do not want to know the reality of the situation. This is a very harmful way to live.

Just because you have a budget does not mean anything has changed. It lets you know the truth, and the truth will set you free. If you do not live in your truth, it will lead to great bondage.

I have lived in the bondage of debt, and it is a nightmare. Even if you feel you do not have enough income, when you know the truth, you can plan accordingly.

The number one money quicksand to watch out for is eating out. It is highly important to budget what you can afford for eating out and no more. You will get into debt faster with this than with any other budget item. Eating out is such a culprit because you think to yourself, "This isn't much to spend on this food," but before you know it, you are over your head in debt, wondering what happened. It is the day-to-day expenses that can add up. Whatever your vice or your addiction of sorts, always give yourself a budget. It will keep you out of the darkness of debt.

An important financial principle from the Bible is tithing. I learned a lot about this principle with Raymon. Raymon and I were deep in debt in the first years of our marriage. I told God that as soon as I got out of debt I would start giving. God showed me His truth. I found out quickly I was starting to have expenses that were hurting my effort to get out of debt. When we give God first what is His, God protects the rest of our money to bless us. God says to give Him at least ten percent of our income.

When I said yes to God and gave to Him first, we started the huge climb out of debt. We went from being one hundred thousand dollars in debt to being debt-free just three years later. We did this while faithfully giving what was owed to the Lord. I have also seen that this will release any barriers of bitterness towards the Lord because of our loss.

SUMMARY

Our physical, emotional, and financial well-being is so important to maintain in order to take control of our lives. There will be a time when you are not in the darkness of your tunnel. I know it does not feel like that now, but in time, and allowing God to heal your heart, you will get out of the tunnel. Focusing on your well-being will help you enormously on the other side. No matter how hard it may be (especially at first), you will be free of excess weight, mental breakdowns, and outstanding debt. You will truly be able to come out a successful person and be free to go and help others through their darkest hours.

Lord Jesus,

I need Your help to take care of myself. I am hurting and my feelings are louder than ever. Please help me to do the right things through my journey in my tunnel. I know You can help me travel easier than if I don't ask for Your help. Help me to find something enjoyable so I can be physically active. Help me not to go overboard in anything, whether eating or shopping. Lord, I trust that one day You are going to heal me completely, and I want to be able to walk out of my tunnel victoriously.

In Jesus' Name,

Amen.

"I Surrender All" is a beloved hymn that continues to encourage me when dealing with all areas of my life. May this song be a daily prayer to surrender your physical, emotional, and financial well-being.

I Surrender All

1 All to Jesus I surrender,
All to Him I freely give;
I will ever love and trust Him,
In His presence daily live.

Refrain:
I surrender all, I surrender all;
All to Thee, my blessed Savior,
I surrender all.

2 All to Jesus I surrender,
Make my, Savior, wholly Thine;
Let me feel Thy Holy Spirit,
Truly know that Thou art mine. [Refrain]

3 All to Jesus I surrender,
Lord, I give myself to Thee;
Fill me with Thy love and power,
Let Thy blessing fall on me. [Refrain]

Judson W. Van DeVenter (1855-1939)

(Public Domain)

MAJOR RAYMON EDWARD GEORGE
On his birthday just four days prior to him going home to Heaven

Chapter XI

Celebrating Memories

The first year of the tunnel may be called "the year of the firsts." There are so many first, ranging from the first time you spend holidays without the one you love, to the many day to day activities such as going to a store or a restaurant without your loved one. Every first in this year can be very hard. For example, the first summer after Raymon went to Heaven I realized I would not see Raymon again in his shorts. This truth hit me as I was walking by the men's shorts in Walmart. I had to hide myself in a secluded area in the store to cry over that truth. He looked good in those shorts.

Every second day of the month was a difficult day. Raymon had passed on March 2 and every monthly anniversary was a reminder of it. It was another month telling me how much time he had been away from me. It was difficult when the yearly time frame of his loss arrived. The last week of February is full of memories. Raymon's last birthday was on Monday and he went to Heaven on Friday.

Christmas was the hardest first with all the decorations and seeing all the couples so warmly celebrating together. It is a long and tough season to get through. Now stores are starting to market their Christmas items in September. I remember seeing the eggnog in the fridge section at Walmart and hiding in the shoe department to cry.

The first birthday without our loved one is difficult. I remember when the special days were over, I breathed a sigh of relief. After the first year, life without our loved one is still hard. The commemorations of our loved one's birthday, anniversary, and their homegoing day continue to be difficult.

One thing I discovered was how there would be a series of many different times of grieving and letting go. I was so surprised to discover how many everyday items or situations brought such pain to my heart. I suppose when we lose our loved one, we realize the great impact they have on almost every detail of our lives. Then there were things I thought would be hard, yet God gave me a lot of grace to get through them. This is a natural part of grief. Every one of us travels through our very own personal tunnel. The important thing is to keep taking the next step and the next.

Through this difficult year and beyond we can celebrate our loved one's life. We can celebrate who they were and all they taught us through their relationship with us. Let us focus on the life they lived instead of their death and what they didn't do. I have dedicated this chapter to how I focused on Raymon's life and offer ideas that may help you in accomplishing this regarding your own loved one. I welcome your feedback on how you personally celebrate your loved one's life. I would love to hear about your celebrations and how you honored your loved one and be able to share it with others.

I cannot emphasize enough the fact that our loved ones are not dead but very much alive. We are eternal beings. We serve an eternal God, and we are made in His image. Even with Raymon not being present in body, he is very much alive in my heart. We had such a deep connection, and I still know how he would respond to things currently happening. I even continue to feel his encouragement when times are very difficult. I am sure your loved one taught you many life lessons. You will carry these with you until you are reunited with them.

Every time we share those lessons with others, it is a celebration of their life. If they could talk to us right now, they would not want us to remember their death or how they came to that death, but rather they would have us celebrate all the days they were alive.

It is so hard when we are grieving to get past those dark last days of their life, but doing certain things will help. Let us focus on honoring our loved ones. There are so many ways in which you can celebrate their lives. One is celebrating those special days that honored them.

Their birthday is a great day to celebrate who they are. I love to honor Raymon in doing those things that made him smile. He loved oldies music, so I will listen to those fifties and sixties oldies and just smile all day. Yes, there are tears that come, but it is like rain on a beautiful sunny day.

For example, whenever I hear the song "The Lion Sleeps Tonight" I remember how he would belt out that song and make me laugh so hard. He would be so into the song and really make the high pitches and the low pitches of the song uniquely his. These types of memories are what our loved ones want desperately for us to remember. They still want to make us smile.

Three years after Raymon's homegoing, I was shopping in Walmart on his birthday. I received a call on my cell phone. The caller hung up before I could answer it. I then called back and found out it was a radio station. I asked if someone there had called me and they said no.

On my way home, I called again and asked what radio station this was. They said they were an AM oldies station. My jaw dropped. I told them I was in Walmart shopping when "somehow" they called me, and I told them my story of how my late husband was a huge oldies fan and this was his birthday. The girl at this small station said she had goose bumps.

She then asked if I would share his story on the air and dedicate a song to him. I said that I would absolutely love to. I got to celebrate my husband that day with a dedication and request his song to me, "My Special Angel". It was incredible!

So for your loved one's birthday, make it a day of remembrance. Invite others to join you in his or her special day. Have a birthday party!!! Have all of his or her favorite food and music. Have the ones you invited bring a special picture. Go around and share what that person taught each of you. When the party is at its end, send a balloon up in the air. Thank God for such a special life that He gave to share with you.

Another great way to honor your loved one is to have a foundation in their name. Many of the foundations we have today were started due to a tragedy in someone's life. The foundation can be based on something that was so meaningful and important to your loved one, or it could be related to others dealing with the same issues your loved one faced. It can be as small or as big as you can handle. It may be a scholarship given in their name to a particular kind of student. College students are very thankful for any assistance towards their obligations.

Another idea is make a special donation to a certain organization or group on the anniversary of the loved one's passing. All of these ideas are special ways to celebrate the life of your loved one. I personally made a special donation to our Teen Challenge group at our church. They were able to purchase a bus for the boys to travel to church as well as travel to other churches to raise support. They placed a memorial dedication to Raymon on the back of the bus.

When I presented the check to Teen Challenge, I shared Raymon's heart to the church and these boys. Raymon had such a heart for boys to grow and be strong men in Christ. Raymon loved to volunteer for the boys' Sunday Schools and camps in the summer. In fact, he was voted best boy's counselor at the last camp he volunteered for. Every time I saw the back of that bus, I would smile.

For those of you that have lost a soldier, Memorial Day is a great day to honor them. I absolutely love going to D.C. and attending the very special concert they have on the Capitol grounds. It is very honoring to all of our soldiers who have given their lives in service to our country. The parade they have around the National Mall is so full of celebration of these lives. You feel the unity between those of us that are left behind. If you have a chance to do this, I encourage you strongly to do it. If you are unable to go to D.C., look in the newspapers for celebrations in your community.

Anniversaries are special days to remember your husband or wife. Raymon and I married on Memorial Day weekend, so it always comes alongside Memorial Day and was a double celebration. I would go to Arlington and take a special arrangement of roses including a red rose for the love we shared, a yellow rose for being my best friend, and a white rose representing the celebration of us being reunited one day. I placed the roses at his headstone. I also took with me his recordings from Iraq. I could not be happier that I had these in my possession. I heard his sweet messages to me and him singing "The Lion Sleeps Tonight" and "My Special Angel". I would laugh and cry. I also brought with me his favorite drink of choice, a Mountain Dew. It was always a very special time.

This may be a time to go to your very special hangout or getaway. You do not necessarily have to go to their cemetery but simply to a special place where you have memories. It could be a park or it could be a special place at the beach. Take with you those special cards or notes they gave you. Take a music player of choice and play *your* songs. Do things that would represent and celebrate your relationship with each other.

Now there may be things they loved that were not your cup of tea. Do not feel as if you have to do these things to honor them. Raymon, for instance, loved roller coasters. He would go on any and all of them. I, on the other hand, do not love roller coasters. I would simply look at them and smile and remember how he looked when he got off of them. He would have his hair blown back a certain way with that special "Oh yeah" smile.

For the rest of your life there are going to be things that you see and hear that will always remind you of your loved one. I encourage you to embrace these sights, sounds, and even smells. Let it be a way for your loved one to bring a smile to your face. Every time I see a helicopter in the sky, I place my hand on my heart and send Raymon my love.

Christmas always makes us think of those we hold so dear in our hearts and those we cannot be with right now. "Holly Jolly Christmas" by Burl Ives will be

Raymon's Christmas song forever. Every time I hear it, I smile and I feel he is telling me, "Merry Christmas." I so loved how he would belt out the song throughout the Christmas season.

What Christmas song do you think of when you think of your loved one? I pray you will feel warmth inside and have a smile on your face knowing they are thinking of you. Another idea to celebrate your loved one at Christmas is place a special ornament on your tree to let them know you are thinking of them.

On Christmas Day, I tell Raymon and my other loved ones in Heaven, "Merry Christmas" and blow them a kiss. Your love for one another will never end.

For those of you who are dealing with the loss of your father or mother, a great day to celebrate their lives is Father's or Mother's Day. Incorporate any of these previous ideas into that day. If you have siblings, it would be a great time to gather together and celebrate. Share your love for your family member and all they meant to you. I know there will be a lot of lessons, recipes, and laughter to share.

You do not need anyone with you to remember and honor your loved one. For the most part I did it on my own. I simply am sharing with you a few ideas that I have found fun and celebratory. I would have enjoyed some of my special days with others more often if it had not been for the distance between us.

Be prepared that some people handle grief and loss differently than others. Some of the people in your life may be very private and closed off. They simply are trying to figure out how to deal with the grief. They may not be ready. Be respectful and understanding. Do not let yourself be angered and hurt by this. Even though they absolutely loved your special one, it simply hurts too much right now for them to participate.

Everyone deals with their grief in their own personal way. Just invite, and if no one shows up, all you need is your personal memories in order to laugh and cry. I celebrated alone many times, and being alone did not take away from the specialness of that day. You, in fact, may be the one who is not ready. This is more than OK. Time does not heal, but it will make a way for you to know how to handle and deal with your grief.

I took a road trip along the East Coast. It was a trip full of memories, but it was another way to process the grief and loss. I began my journey in Savannah where I was invited to attend a change of command ceremony. The one accepting the new command was Raymon's and my friend Stuart. Raymon took command from Stuart at Fort Eustis, Virginia right before I met Raymon. Stuart and his wife were dear friends of ours during our dating time. We asked them to be in our wedding. This is the same couple I mentioned whom I saw again at Arlington the day we laid Raymon's body to rest.

After attending the change of command ceremony, I then took my sweet time and made my way up the coast. I stayed in the Charleston area for a night. I stayed for a night in Carolina Beach, the area where we honeymooned. I even went to the Fort Fisher campgrounds where we stayed. It put a big smile on my face to see it again, army tanks and all.

I went down to the beach where I remembered we took some pictures together by the North Carolina Aquarium. It was a way of remembering and letting go. I continued up the coast until I came to my hometown of Newport News, Virginia. It was such a therapeutic trip. I suggest that for closure, you go to those special places that have great memories or go to places you said you always wanted to go together.

You know the special days that meant so much to you and your loved one. You can choose to make these days all that you want them to be. Make them as simple or as big as you like. Just keep in mind, the most important thing to remember is that your special someone wants you to "Smile!!!".

When I was headed to the airport, visiting Raymon for the last time in D.C., the song "I Will Rise" by Chris Tomlin came on the radio just as I was passing by Arlington National Cemetery. It was perfect timing! It reminded me of the ultimate celebration I will have with Raymon when we are together again. Until then I will celebrate his life here and know he would want me to celebrate knowing he is indeed free and in no more pain. He is with Jesus!

CHAPTER XII

The Golden Key

It is so important not to be an island away from others. We need each other. God always intended His children to be unified and help encourage each other along life's journey. You have a time for others to reach out to you, and then there is a time for you to help others. We all have our purpose in this journey to be a source of life-giving help.

Friends and Family Give Strength

⁹ Two people are better than one,
because they get more done
by working together.

¹⁰ If one falls down, the other
can help him up.
But it is bad for the person
who is alone and falls,
because no one is there to help.

Ecclesiastes 4:9-10 (NCV)

I have a difficult time asking friends and family for help when I feel God and I can handle it together. I see people with their own problems and families to take care of, and I do not want to be an extra burden. However, I have discovered that people like to be a blessing.

There is a balance between being needy and asking for help. We are to do what we can handle, but it is OK to share your need for help when you do. Do not keep trying to do something with no results. Ask. Do not let pride stand in the way if you are in need of help.

If someone does not know the answer or what to do, they usually will help you with trying to find someone that can help. Be open to whomever God may use to be a vessel of blessing. Stay connected with your church.

You may have to attend a church group you may not expect. When I started going to a new church after Raymon passed, I didn't know which group I should join. I wanted to have some social connection, but I found out they did not have a singles group for those my age and older.

Unfortunately, a lot of churches fail to take care of the older singles. I ended up attending a singles group which included those as young as eighteen and ended at my age of thirty-five.

This was an interesting dynamic, but it is all I had to choose from. I did not feel that I totally belonged, but I just made the best of what I had. The Lord gave me some special friends in that group.

I also enjoyed being a part of Toastmasters, a group that teaches you leadership and speaking skills. I enjoyed the diverse array of people in the group. We had a wide range of ages and backgrounds to learn from. I always enjoyed the speeches that were presented. I felt very encouraged when it was my time to present my speech. For the most part, you were assigned a different role at each meeting. For example, some of the roles were Timer, "uh" counter, Evaluator, and Grammarian. These roles changed weekly so it made the meeting always interesting as we met twice a month. I enjoyed the socialization, and my speaking skills improved as well.

Try to join groups that share your interests. Here are some options to help you. You can usually research these online and find out if there are any in your area.

Social Groups
- Book club
- Golf group
- Bowling League
- Karaoke place
- Senior Centers, if applicable
- Toastmasters
- College class (a great way to learn something and be social)
- Dance class (my best friend loves to line dance and teaches it)
- Sports team, such as a softball team
- Travel club

- Cooking club
- Equestrian club
- Fishing pier (this isn't an official club, but if you consistently go to the same pier you will develop relationships)

It is so important to have a great balance of being with people to meet your needs and being a vessel God can use to help others.

I will never forget how my youth pastor gave this wonderful illustration describing this balance. The person that was doing all the giving was a scrawny, withdrawn person, to the point they were all shriveled up. The person that did all the taking was this big, huge, blown-up person that was so big they were no good to anyone. There is a great flow to and from a healthy person. They are receiving and they are giving.

You will be healthy when you open yourself to receive from the Lord, which can be done by spending time with Him and receiving from others. Then God will give you wonderful opportunities to bless others. As you allow yourself to be a vessel of blessing, your soul will become healthier and strong.

The best way to be healed along the road of grief is by reaching out to others. Just as I suggested that you go and experience a Holocaust museum or movie, there are others who are suffering just as much or worse than you. To remain in our pain and grief without reaching out will suck us into a deep pit of self-pity and depression.

Your pain need not be in vain. This was the greatest joy to come to me through my pain of loss. The Lord showed me that with my pain came the golden key of ministry. People were opening up to me in ways I had never seen. People have told me in the past they could talk to me, but this was a whole new level in ministry to people's hearts.

When people found out about my loss, they were opening up and sharing their own pain with me. In fact, I had a woman share with me something she said she had told no one for seventeen years. She said there was no one else she felt comfortable sharing her deep pain with before. I felt so humbled by her openness to me.

When I sat in a restaurant, especially by myself, I had servers at restaurants open up about their pain. Even though people do not experience the same kind of loss, they know that you know what pain is. When they realize your pain experience, they will open up to you. God desires for you to take this awesome responsibility as a blessing of ministry and use it to bring others to Him.

One big example of this is when I was asked at my church to be a part of the jail ministry. I knew God was saying yes for me to go. I was asked to be the leader after a couple of times of visiting. The imprisoned women looked at me as if to say, "What do you have to give us?" Their faces were stern and hardened. They must have felt that since I came in my nice church clothes and smiled sweetly, I would have nothing to say to them that would relate to their situation.

Once I finished sharing my testimony, I could see visible changes in their countenances. They were ready and willing to receive the message I came to give. My message was this: "The Lord wants you to give your pain to Him. You are in that jail cell because you chose to deal with your pain in your own way. God wants to set you free. Learn to deal with your pain God's way. Once you receive that freedom that Jesus died to give you, you can use your testimony to help others be free too." This brought them hope and excitement. They desperately needed hope and purpose, and Jesus was there to offer it to them. I absolutely loved those women and I felt like I was walking on air every time I left because of the freedom they were receiving in their lives. This I knew put a smile on Jesus' face.

Soon after the entrance into my tunnel of grief, a dear friend of the family told me something that still excites me to this day.

God was showing her that I was going to use the same sword the enemy came after me with to cut his head off. David had done the same with Goliath. The passage when David speaks to Goliath is found in 1 Samuel 17.

45 Then said David to the Philistine, You come to me with a sword, a spear, and a javelin, but I come to you in the name of

the Lord of hosts, the God of the ranks of Israel, Whom you have defied. ⁴⁶ This day the Lord will deliver you into my hand, and I will smite you and cut off your head. And I will give the corpses of the army of the Philistines this day to the birds of the air and the wild beasts of the earth, that all the earth may know that there is a God in Israel. ⁴⁷ And all this assembly shall know that the Lord saves not with sword and spear; for the battle is the Lord's, and He will give you into our hands.

1 Samuel 17:45-47 (AMP)

Every time God gives me the opportunity to share my testimony and it gives others hope to seek God for their healing, I am doing just that. Let me tell you, it feels— Great!!! God has bestowed to you a personalized, handcrafted, golden key of ministry. It will unlock the hearts of people who have their pain and wounds so locked inside. What a great privilege!

³ Praise be to the God and Father of our Lord Jesus Christ, the Father of compassion and the God of all comfort, ⁴ who comforts us in all our troubles, so that we can comfort those in any trouble with the comfort we ourselves receive from God. ⁵ For just as

> **we share abundantly in the sufferings of Christ, so also our comfort abounds through Christ.**
>
> *2 Corinthians 1:3-5 (NIV)*

I was with my mom in Newport News shopping when I got a call. This call came the October after Raymon went home to Heaven. It was one of the women from PWOC. She said she had done a lot of praying and kept asking God who should be the stage director for the upcoming Southeast Regional Conference. She said my face was the only one that kept coming to her.

At first, I was a bit shocked that I was asked. Also, I was shocked because I had no interest in attending the conference at all. I did not want to be surrounded by five hundred-plus happily married military wives. I knew the Lord had set me up and I knew He had a plan, so I accepted the position. It was a job with great responsibility. I drove to Franklin, Tennessee where it would be held.

Having the job as stage director, I was responsible for the flow of each of the six general sessions. Each session had praise and worship, an artist, an actress who performed spoken word, and our main speaker. Our special musical guest was Kathy Troccoli. I could not believe the Lord said that not only was I going to this event, but also that I was going to organize and direct the event. I also was given the opportunity to create a powerful drama to drive home the overall theme for the conference. God opened doors that were above and beyond what I could ever imagine or think.

It was a very challenging role, but it was an outstanding experience. I know that this experience is going to be so helpful for my new ministry, which I'll talk about in the next chapter. At this conference, I met the directors of Military Ministry, a division of Campus Crusade for Christ.

I worked with Military Ministry for the next couple of years. I was able to talk to many people about Raymon's sacrifice and share about a ministry that had wonderful resources for soldiers and their families. It was a challenge at times, but overall it was a great experience. The biggest fulfillment was when I was able to share and counsel with soldiers and their wives one on one.

One of my very first experiences with Military Ministry was when a group of us flew to Fort Hood to lead a couple's retreat. One of the blessings I received was seeing my dear friend Suzanne, and it was on my birthday. She is the friend who drove out from Texas to be with me right after Raymon entered Heaven.

Our first night started out with a spaghetti dinner for the couples, and I was assigned to be available wherever the Lord led me. I asked the Lord where I should sit after I got my spaghetti. The Lord showed me this couple, and I asked to sit down. Their faces were so sad and sullen, almost to the point of being very uncomfortable. I began with small talk. I then felt led to share my testimony with them. What happened next was, to me, a miracle. Those hard faces began to have tears streaming down them. I looked at both of them and realized God had allowed me to use my golden key to unlock their hearts.

They opened up to me that they didn't even want to come to the couple's seminar, and they were on the verge of a divorce. The Lord impressed on me to tell them there is hope. There is hope!!!

I found out he was dealing with severe PTSD, and it was really doing damage to their marriage. He opened up to me, and I was able to counsel him. She told me on the side that he did not talk to anyone, and she was so happy he was opening up to me. They attended every part of the weekend couple's retreat when they originally said they didn't know if they would make it through the first night. I smiled and hugged them every time I saw them. I poured into them the love and hope that Jesus had poured into me.

One of the couples I worked with in Texas kept in touch with the couple who had been near divorce. Whenever the Texas couple talked to me, they shared how the once-hurting couple was still together and working things out. God wants to use your testimony to bring great hope and victory to people's lives. Be obedient even when it feels uncomfortable at times.

Let us pray:

Dear Jesus,

I want to be healthy when it comes to people. I do admit my need to receive from those You place into my life. You have created me to need relationships and I ask that they would be healthy relationships. Help me to have courage to let go of the unhealthy relationships I have allowed. I want to be a vessel You can use even in this darkest hour of my life. I do not want my pain to be in vain. I now receive my golden key of ministry. I realize there are so many people hurting around me. Lord, may I have Your words of life and hope to give to them. Let me be transparent enough to share my testimony. Thank You for all the wonderful experiences You have in store in my future.

In Jesus' Name, Amen.

"Make Me a Channel of Your Peace" is a song that summarizes the heart of this chapter.

Weeping may endure for a night, But a shout of joy comes in the morning. Psalm 30:5b (AMP)

"Before The Morning" by Josh Wilson is a song that reminds me of this truth. May it encourage you!

CHAPTER XIII

Beckoning Light

> "For I know the plans I have for you," declares the LORD, "plans to prosper you and not to harm you, plans to give you hope and a future."
>
> *Jeremiah 29:11 (NIV)*

The first time I saw this verse was when I was a child, in the kid's room at my grandparent's house. I had taken the Bible and prayed to God that He would reveal something special just for me. I closed my eyes and placed my finger randomly in the Bible. I somehow feel God honored my prayer that day, especially with my child-like faith.

This verse gives me great hope. I had a friend who, shortly after Raymon went home to Heaven, shared the verse with me often. Frankly, I was not in the mood to hear it then. God knows what we need to hear even when our emotions are in an upheaval. Even though I didn't want to hear it, I knew down deep it was true.

I have shared with you how God used my testimony to help people. This has been a great blessing and is only the start of His plan for me. The Lord gave me the time to grieve, and my time in grief was exactly like a tunnel. Even when I saw the light, I still had more of the tunnel to travel through. God showed me a little piece of the puzzle at a time. He showed me just enough to give me hope and a little sneak peek of what He had in store. This truth is beautifully illustrated on the cover of this book. Believe me, I wanted so desperately for more of the picture, but I truly believe God does not show us everything because He knows we would be tempted to try to take control and try to work things out for ourselves and eventually mess it all up.

Amazing Grace

I decided to go on eHarmony in March of 2010. I felt a peace about doing this and actually a little spiritual nudge in that direction. I really desired to have some companionship and a coffee buddy. I met a couple of men I was matched up with and they were very nice, but that spark simply was not there. And then it happened, on June 10, 2010. I was matched up with a man named Scott from Fayetteville, Georgia. This was the first time I was matched with someone in my local area. His profile was very interesting and I liked what it said.

He was a Christian. He loved to sing. I quickly noticed two of the songs he sang were "Be Still and Know" and "I Can Only Imagine," two very meaningful songs God gave me early in my journey in my tunnel.

I went through the required levels of messaging, and he responded in kind. What usually takes two people about a week or more to work through, we finished in one day. He emailed me a couple of days later and asked if we could meet. I was overjoyed! In my spirit I felt God was saying, "*This is the one!*" I told God, "We will see about that." Even though I wanted someone in my life to do things with, I wasn't sure if I was really ready for a serious relationship. I was very guarded.

We chose to meet for a pre-date at our local coffee spot. It was Wednesday, June 16. We sat down on the nice leather sofa and began to talk. He had the most beautiful eyes, and it was easy to make eye contact while talking. He was very friendly and warm. To be honest, I still was not convinced where this would go. I could see us being friends for sure.

Our first real date was the following day, and we met at my favorite Chinese restaurant. He still was very friendly and I could tell he loved to communicate. This was so very different from Raymon. I asked him if he would like to go to a karaoke spot where I had been a few times. I was a little sneaky about this because I really wanted to see if he could truly sing. If this was to go anywhere, I wanted to be able to tell the truth when asked, "Did you like my song?"

The moment came an hour later when he began to sing "Home" by Michael Bublé. I smiled from ear to ear. He did indeed know how to sing and it sounded very good. I sang "The Rose" by Bette Midler and he enjoyed my singing. We even did a silly duet together. The song did not go very well but was fun. At the end of the night we hugged quickly and said goodnight.

The following night, a Friday, we decided to meet for dinner and go bowling. The funniest thing happened. He bowled a turkey (three strikes in a row) in frames seven through nine on our first game. This was very impressive. In the next game, I bowled a turkey in frames seven through nine. This completely surprised me because I just don't bowl turkeys. We sat down and talked over ice cream in their café. We talked about some in-depth things we were looking for in our future mates. I was finding it very easy to talk to him even about more serious things.

I explained to him the two very important items on my hand and wrist. The blue ribbon had been on my wrist since my time in Mannheim when I was in the "Believing God" Bible study. It symbolized to me that I believe God in all areas of my life. The wedding band on my left ring finger had been worn since April 8, 2007 on Easter morning. It symbolized that God had been my husband since Raymon went to Heaven.

I really appreciated that Scott respected Raymon and the fact that I was a military widow. He did not get scared off like so many other men I had encountered along my journey, and he tried to understand as much as he could. Our next date was for the following Monday.

On Sunday at church I went down for prayer. My pastor prayed with me, and all of a sudden he gave me a word that God was going to bring the man He wanted to give me—soon. My pastor was even a bit shocked about delivering this word to me. He is not one to give out words readily, so I knew it was indeed from God. He had no idea I was beginning to see Scott. He even said to me, "Amy, I don't know why God is having me say this to you right now." I was thinking, "Daddy God, you really want to get this message to me about Scott."

The next night, on Monday, we met at a movie called *My Family Wedding*. It was the best lighthearted movie playing in the theaters at the time, but what another sign! We were both feeling a little irritable. Scott was tired, and I was feeling a bit oppressed. I was having the opportunity for ministry quite often now with Military Ministry. The enemy was not happy about it, and he was trying to steal my peace and joy.

At dinner, Scott let me know he wanted to pray for me later in the evening. This was so sweet, and I was so encouraged that he offered. Later that evening, we were sitting at his kitchen counter by a big bay window. There must have been hundreds of fireflies blinking their lights. It was such an amazing sight. Scott laid his hand on my shoulder and began to pray a beautiful prayer for me. He then began to sing "Who Am I" by Casting Crowns. He sang more powerful and anointed than ever before. This singing outdid his karaoke singing by far. Then he sang "Be Still and Know" by Steven Curtis Chapman. I immediately broke down in tears. No man has ever sung to me a God song like this. *Be Still and Know* were the first words God spoke to me right before I found out Raymon went home to Heaven, and now Scott was singing those very words. The meaning of the song was God's heart to me, and He was using Scott's voice to bring the message once again.

We decided to sing a duet to see how we would sound together. We sang "Amazing Grace." When we got done singing, there was this amazing feeling in the room. I have never sung a more beautiful duet. I started saying to God in my spirit, "You may be right." After a little time at Scott's house, he came over to my house to have a tour. I shared with him the story about my window and how I greet Daddy God there every morning. I also told him about the first morning back as a widow and how God lovingly told me to come and rest in Him. Next thing I knew, Scott grabbed my granny's Bible that I had sitting on my nightstand and said, "I want to share something with you that God is laying on my heart." He laid the Bible on my bed and turned to Psalm 139. He had no idea, but that very spot where he laid the Bible was the place I had said my last goodbye to Raymon the morning I left for Virginia. Scott began to read:

O Lord, You have searched me and known me.
² You know my sitting down and my rising up; You understand my thought afar off.

³ You comprehend my path and my lying down, And are acquainted with all my ways.

⁴ For there is not a word on my tongue, But behold, O Lord, You know it altogether.

⁵ You have hedged me behind and before, And laid Your hand upon me.

⁶ Such knowledge is too wonderful for me; It is high, I cannot attain it.

⁷ Where can I go from Your Spirit? Or where can I flee from Your presence?

⁸ If I ascend into heaven, You are there; If I make my bed in hell, behold, You are there.

⁹ If I take the wings of the morning, And dwell in the uttermost parts of the sea,

¹⁰ Even there Your hand shall lead me, And Your right hand shall hold me.

¹¹ If I say, "Surely the darkness shall fall on me," Even the night shall be light about me;

¹² Indeed, the darkness shall not hide from You, But the night shines as the day; The darkness and the light are both alike to You.

¹³ For You formed my inward parts; You covered me in my mother's womb.

¹⁴ I will praise You, for I am fearfully and wonderfully made; Marvelous are Your works, And that my soul knows very well.

¹⁵ My frame was not hidden from You, When I was made in secret, And skillfully wrought in the lowest parts of the earth.

¹⁶ Your eyes saw my substance, being yet unformed. And in Your book they all were written, The days fashioned for me, When as yet there were none of them.

¹⁷ How precious also are Your thoughts to me, O God! How great is the sum of them!

¹⁸ If I should count them, they would be more in number than the sand; When I awake, I am still with You.

¹⁹ Oh, that You would slay the wicked, O God! Depart from me, therefore, you bloodthirsty men.

²⁰ For they speak against You wickedly; Your enemies take Your name in vain.

²¹ Do I not hate them, O LORD, who hate You? And do I not loathe those who rise up against You?

²² I hate them with perfect hatred; I count them my enemies.

²³ Search me, O God, and know my heart; Try me, and know my anxieties;

²⁴ And see if there is any wicked way in me, And lead me in the way everlasting.

Psalm 139 (NKJV)

When Scott read this beautiful passage of scripture, he had tears running down his face. He had a love of God and His word like I had never seen in a man before. I was beginning to see what God had seen all along.

We continued dating for the next year and had an amazing dating relationship. Scott was very attentive and expressed how much he enjoyed being with me. Our relationship was very pure. Some people may find that surprising, because for some reason there are those who feel that once you have been married or reached a certain age, purity in a relationship is not expected or required by God, or people may have a "God will understand" attitude.

Scott was an amazing man that respected me, and frankly himself, in a Christian relationship. It was wonderful and refreshing. Scott and I shared many of the same interests and hobbies.

Scott is the first man that actually played a game called the Ungame with me. It isn't a typical game but really an activity with lots of questions that allows the players to really get to know one another. I highly recommend it for getting to know someone in all the different areas of their life.

Our particular game was the Christian version, so it also included separate questions that had to do with your spiritual walk. We played this game in the first several months of our relationship, and I really appreciated and liked the answers Scott was giving me.

We enjoyed a lot of the same kind of activities, especially singing. We went to a golf course club to do most of our karaoke singing. We were the babies of the group. They loved on us and enjoyed watching our love blossom. Scott and I sang love songs to each other. We were really sappy I suppose. They had dancing as well, and we enjoyed slow dancing to songs that our friends would dedicate to us. One of our favorite singers and friends was Tom, a retired principal who was eighty-plus years old. He would sing the classic ballads from the forties and fifties. His voice was such a delight to listen to. We lost him to Heaven not too long ago.

Scott and I enjoyed traveling, and we loved experiencing new places and different restaurants. I so enjoyed Scott's company. We both are very sociable people, and we have met so many wonderful people along our journey. This quality in Scott was so attractive because this was the first relationship I had been in in which both of us enjoyed getting to know new people and did it with such ease.

Our travels led us to Chicago for our one-year anniversary. We took a tour on top of their open-air bus. Chicago was more beautiful than I ever imagined. We went up, up, up on the elevator of the tallest building in Chicago. I held close to Scott on that ride. It was such a beautiful day for our one-year anniversary that I was wondering if Scott would propose, but he did not.

The next day we went to the Navy Pier and had so much fun! There was a lot to see and it was up close and personal to the water. I love the water, especially since I grew up around it, and now I was living in landlocked Atlanta. We took our time making our way down the pier. They had a beautiful stained glass exhibit. We finally made our way to the end and saw the beautiful view with a lighthouse sitting out in the middle of the water.

Next thing I knew Scott began to share with me how he had enjoyed our relationship. He shared with me how I inspired him to be a better man. Before I could catch my breath, he said, "Amy, will you marry me?" He opened a ring box with a beautiful princess-cut diamond ring inside. My head was spinning. I had him say it again. I said, "Yes." Scott gave me a moment to speak to my Daddy God. It was time for me to remove my wedding band I wore to honor the fact that Daddy God was my husband, and I praised and thanked Him for all of His faithfulness to me. Scott slipped my new engagement ring on my finger.

My soon-to-be husband was a graduate of Clearwater Christian College with a Bachelor of Science in Bible with a concentration in Church Ministries. Scott had performed in many community theater plays. He was from a very musical family whose talent is amazing. Most importantly, Scott was raised in a God centered home. God knew the plan all along. Thus He said, *Be still and know I am God.* The Lord *is* my Redeemer.

I wish I could tell you there was nothing but happiness after our engagement. The truth is there was a time when a part of me did not understand how I could move on. Raymon and I had not divorced. We were happily married. I asked some very close friends of mine to pray for me. I wanted to move on, but there was a part of my heart that did not understand how I could.

During prayer time, one of the ladies said, "You must let go of Raymon." I started to weep. I told the Lord I didn't understand how I could. The Lord sweetly told me I was not breaking my commitment to Raymon. He took me to the altar where we married and said, *"Amy, your vow was not broken but has been made complete. You were faithful to your vow. It is complete. Well done."* God had given me the gift of His perspective.

<u>Wedding Day</u>

The morning of November 5, 2011 had arrived. It was my wedding day! We chose the fifth because the number five stands for grace. God's amazing grace was indeed working in our lives. It was a beautiful day. My sister came to my bedroom door to greet me and say, "Happy Wedding Day!" I have to admit I was not the innocent, blissful bride. I knew this was a huge day, and I was making a very serious commitment. I knew what marriage was, and I knew even though there is great satisfaction in having a lifelong partner, it takes a lot of work and commitment.

I had been widowed for four years and eight months. It had been a very long, hard road. As I stood in my bridal room awaiting my walk down the aisle, the song "While I'm Waiting" by John Waller began to play. This song ministered so deeply to my heart during the journey in my tunnel; it had become my anthem. I would serve the Lord through all the difficulties and await a day like today. When the song played, I was overwhelmed with emotion and thanksgiving to the Lord. He had been so faithful through all of my widowhood.

I would no longer be a widow but a married woman once again. I raised my arms to the Lord as I looked towards this beautiful stained glass window. I praised Him throughout the song. God is faithful!

Standing with arms held high to God while "While I'm Waiting" plays at our wedding.

"Agnus Dei" began to play. My sister looked out the door and then at me saying, "You have a very handsome man waiting for you." She preceded me down the aisle. I was so thankful she would be standing beside me in this very important day. Though my dad had escorted me down the aisle in my wedding with Raymon, I felt in my heart and spirit I wanted my Heavenly Father to escort me down the aisle this time. I felt His presence all the way as I carried one white rose with my bouquet of red roses down the aisle. I placed the white rose, tied with the blue ribbon I had cut off my wrist earlier that day, into a vase to honor Raymon. This symbolized letting go of Raymon's hand and joining hands with Scott.

Letting go of Raymon's hand and joining hands with Scott

It was a very beautiful ceremony. Scott shared a few words before he sang his surprise song to me—"Love of My Life" by Michael W. Smith. He had no idea what this song meant to me. I remember one of the times flying home to Virginia, after Raymon passed away, looking out at the sky and listening to this very song— praying one day a man would sing this song to me.

After Scott sang to me, I shared with him about a very special time when God comforted me during my first trip back to Arlington to visit Raymon's grave. I said to Scott, "God spoke to my heart that He would bless me once again with a very special gift, and that gift is you!" The music for my surprise song to Scott began, and I sang "I Won't Let Go" by Rascal Flatts.

After our pastor pronounced us as husband and wife, we sang "Amazing Grace" together in our wedding as our first duet as husband and wife. At the end of our wedding we asked for our guests to join us at the altar to stand together and pray for us. Through several of their prayers, God declared He was pleased with our union, and He has great plans for our future.

For I Know The Plans

Scott and Amy Birchfield

God spoke to me very clearly through His Word, in that hotel room in Washington D.C., right after we laid Raymon's body to rest in Arlington:

> "The Spirit of the
> Lord God is upon Me,
> Because the Lord has anointed Me
> To preach good tidings to the poor;
> He has sent Me to heal the brokenhearted,
> To proclaim liberty to the captives,
> And the opening of the prison to those who are bound;"
>
> *Isaiah 61:1 (NKJV)*

I have been called to minister to the brokenhearted, and thus I am now pursuing certification in grief counseling. God has called me to use my Golden Key of Ministry. I am so very thankful!

Final Encouragement

Right now it may be really dark for you. I know what that darkness is like. I have been through the tunnel of grief and loss. I am standing at the end of the tunnel shouting words of hope and encouragement to you. Keep going! The light is up ahead-I promise you! Where you are is not the ending. There is MORE!!! There is so much more ahead of you. It may not be a formal full-time ministry, but we all have a purpose God wants us to fulfill. God has placed gifts and talents within all of us to use for His glory. God can use your story to encourage so many others if you surrender yourself and your pain to Him. Do not let the enemy win! Keep pressing forward to Jesus. He will indeed show you the way!

People need you and your story. There may be special people whose road may intersect with yours. Their story along with yours may be such a testimony to this world. These special people awaiting you may be an adopted child. God may fill the mom and dad place in your heart and life with an older woman or man who needs your assistance and all that you may have inside of you to offer. One of the most beautiful things I have experienced in my life is when God intersects my life with that of other special people. These people may even grow to be closer to you than your own original family.

Don't get stuck!!! Jesus said come to Him as a little child. Children have a great ability to bounce back from things. They rebound in ways that are amazing! As adults, we tend to get weary and give up. When I say give up, I am not talking about only physical death but an attitude that says, "Let me lie down in my current circumstances no matter how dismal this feels or how my circumstances may be." God is always up to doing new things in our lives if we will cooperate. We may fool ourselves when we think we are lying still, but in reality, we are moving forward or we are falling backwards.

A great way to illustrate this is to imagine you are standing in the ocean looking out at the shore. You think you are standing in the same area, but the next thing you know, you look for your lounging area and realize it is down the beach much farther than you realized. This life is like the water's current. I pray you will choose to go forward in cooperation with God.

I was ministering to someone just recently about the fact there are only two paths to choose to walk on in this life. There is the God path or there is the Self path. On the Self path there is going to be lots of worry, anxiety, uncertainty, and pain which leads to a Dead End. When we are on the God path, it will lead us to true life which includes all the wonderful plans God has for us. God's plans for us are always filled with God's best for us. We also can release all the burdens of our lives to Him over and over on this path. The astounding thing is that God gave us the choice. I pray with all of my heart that you will choose the God path. I pray you will choose in the midst of your tunnel of loss the path that leads to life. This path leads to Eternal Life. God never intended for you to give up on your journey. He wants all of us to take His hand and let Him guide us all the way home.

> **"I have told you these things, so that in me you may have peace. In this world you will have trouble. But take heart! I have overcome the world."**
>
> *John 16:33 (NIV)*

Jesus died for you to have life and have it more abundantly. The enemy's purpose is the very opposite.

> **The thief's purpose is to steal and kill and destroy. My purpose is to give them a rich and satisfying life.**
>
> *John 10:10 (NLT)*

This is the way you defeat the enemy of darkness:

> **And they have defeated him by the blood of the Lamb and by their testimony.**
>
> *Revelation 12:11a (NLT)*

There are a couple of sayings that are true. We do not become overcomers until we have something to overcome. We do not have a testimony until we have a test. God is there to empower you to overcome so you have a powerful testimony. If you allow God to use this in your life, you will be victorious. You will also be a beacon of light to those still in their dark tunnels of grief and pain.

Please keep moving forward one step at a time. One day at a time. You will start seeing glimmers of light. You will start hearing the sounds of hope. You will see at the end of your tunnel, Jesus! He was with you the whole time carrying you through. He will place you on your feet, look you tenderly in your eyes and say,

"For I always knew the plans I had for you."

"I waited patiently for the Lord to help me, and he turned to me and heard my cry. He lifted me out of the pit of despair, out of the mud and the mire. He set my feet on solid ground and steadied me as I walked along. He has given me a new song to sing, a hymn of praise to our God. Many will see what he has done and be amazed. They will put their trust in the Lord. I take joy in doing your will, my God, for your instructions are written on my heart."

(Psalms 40:1-3, 8 NLT)

I am so thankful I have had the opportunity to walk with you on your journey through the tunnel of loss. As I prayed about how to end this book, the Lord put on my heart what the true light at the end of the tunnel is. There are many false assumptions as to what the light at the end of the tunnel is. The light at the end of the tunnel is Jesus. He is the Great I AM! He is everything we need or will ever need. He is hope. He is life. He is joy. He is peace. He is perfect in every way. Most of all, He is Love. He is perfect love.

The faster we realize He truly is all that we need and will ever need, the faster our darkness in our tunnel will become brighter and brighter. The dependence we have on Jesus Christ is equivalent to the light we will have within our tunnels. Then eventually we will be free of the tunnel and completely living inside the freedom Jesus has for us and died for us to have.

There was a reverend and famous gospel song writer named Thomas Dorsey (1899-1993) who knew the pain of great loss. In the very hour he was leading a church service, he received a telegram that his wife had died in child birth and the very next day the baby also went to Heaven. His lack of understanding and trust in God led him to refuse to write another song. A week later, he was sitting at his friend's piano when the Lord washed over him with great peace. He responded to the Lord in writing a beloved song that concludes our journey together. My concluding prayer for you is that this will be your song and prayer.

Precious Lord, take my hand
Lead me on, let me stand
I am tired, I am weak, I am worn
Through the storm, through the night
Lead me on to the light
Take my hand precious Lord, lead me home

Thomas Dorsey, writer

Hold on to Jesus' hand as He leads you through your tunnel into the light. I can assure you the Light is amazing!

> **I know the Lord is always with me. I will not be shaken, for he is right beside me.**
>
> **You will show me the way of life, granting me the joy of your presence and the pleasures of living with you forever.**
>
> *Psalm 16:8,11 (NLT)*

Heddie,

P.S. I Love You
&
I am praying for you!

Trust in *and* rely confidently on the LORD with all your heart
And do not rely on your own insight or understanding.
6 In all your ways know *and* acknowledge *and* recognize Him,
And He will make your paths straight *and* smooth [removing obstacles that block your way].

Proverbs 3:5-6 (AMP)

Amy Birchfield

My Sister - I love you ♡

ABOUT THE AUTHOR

Amy Birchfield began her journey through the tunnel of loss when her husband Major Raymon George went to Heaven on March 2, 2007. They had suffered with two plus years of severe PTSD after Raymon returned home from his tour in Iraq in Operation Iraqi Freedom. God has given Amy a heart to encourage and inspire others who are traveling through their own tunnels of loss through grief counseling and inspirational speaking. Amy lives currently in the Atlanta, Georgia area.

Printed in the United States
By Bookmasters

Printed in the United States
By Bookmasters